CALIFORNIA'S TOP 10 WINES

By
Alexander Mackenzie

Armstrong Publishing Co.
Los Angeles

CALIFORNIA'S TOP 10 WINES
by Alexander Mackenzie

First printing June 1978
Copyright © 1978 by Armstrong Publishing Company
Library of Congress Catalog Card Number: 78-52685
ISBN: 0-915936-09-7
Printed in the United States of America

Designed By: Augie Rinaldi

Published By: Armstrong Publishing Company
               5514 Wilshire Boulevard
               Los Angeles, California 90036
               (213) 937-3600

TABLE OF CONTENTS

CALIFORNIA WINE: AN INTRODUCTION

Wine has been the stuff of legend for so long that it has become too easy to forget that it exists principally for one reason — to be enjoyed. It is simply a great pleasure, and easy to become acquainted with.

Grapes are a tidy package — sugar inside, yeast on the outside (on the skins) — everything you need to make wine all there. Man intervenes, squeezes them, lets the juice ferment, and bottles the result. Being gifted with curiosity, opposing thumbs and more sensual awareness than other beasts, we have of course tidied up the process and introduced some ingenious wrinkles into the whole business, but we shouldn't lose sight of the basic simplicity of it all. Benjamin Franklin thought it was God's way of recycling water into a more palatable form, by running it through the grape.

People are sometimes put off or even intimidated by the arcane language, rituals and pretensions of connoisseurs and wine snobs, who seem to inhabit ivory towers well-stocked with choice vintages and talk of nothing else. But the wines such people rhapsodize about represent less than ten percent of all the wine drunk around the world every day, and those millions of people who are consuming the everyday stuff are undoubtedly quite happy, as they should be.

I. In the Beginning ...

Wine has been made in California for over 200 years. Franciscan missionaries, led by Padre Junipero Serra, planted grapes as they established a chain of missions up what came to be called El Camino Real, The King's Highway, from San Diego to Sonoma.

In the early 1800s, Spain's grip on this faraway colony weakened, and the missions were abandoned. The melting-pot aspect of California's wine business was soon evident, as a Frenchman began a large vineyard and winery in Los Angeles, Germans did the same in Anaheim, and Italians seemingly did it everywhere else. The Gold Rush of 1849 was the second great wave of immigration, and many names we see on labels today were part of it.

One was a Hungarian, Agoston Haraszthy, and he was the Johnny Appleseed of the wine business, bringing over 100,000 grapevine cuttings from Europe and distributing them all over the state. He was also a little sloppy about record-keeping, and much of the misnaming of grapes which still causes confusion to Europeans began around this time.

The first of several disasters that have broken the progress of wine in America struck a while later. The root louse phylloxera ravaged the vineyards of the state, and evenutally the world. Whole vineyards were dug up and the vines burned. Other crops were planted in many cases. A solution was finally found — phylloxera couldn't abide the native American grapevine species, *vitis labrusca*.

Today, most of the vineyards of the world are planted with the European species *vitis vinifera* grafted onto the rootstock of the American labrusca. The disruption changed the patterns of California viticulture, however; Los Angeles and Anaheim developed into roaring boom towns in the interim, and the action took place further north, in the fog-cooled valleys around San Francisco and the warm reaches of the San Joaquin Valley.

California winemakers were again hitting their stride when a worse disaster struck: Prohibition. Paying a mad and bizarre homage to our Puritan forefathers, we went dry for fifteen years. Once again, grapevines were pulled up or abandoned; even worse, some were replanted in varieties that were thick-skinned and could be shipped East as table grapes, so that when the blessed relief of Repeal came along, there were few proper varieties available for wine.

That break of nearly a generation resulted in an ignorance of wine and its enjoyable uses and merits that lasted many years longer, persisting even till today.

With comparative peace and prosperity upon us after World War II, wine began making a comeback. European travel, first in khaki and then in civilian clothes, introduced many people to wine. The good life became an ideal, and wine was part of it. And in California, it was getting better in a hurry.

The University of California at Davis had started an enology department (enology is the study of wine, broadly) right after Repeal; ten years later, enough of its graduates were working in the field to reshape California winemaking. The small but growing band of consumers who appreciated their efforts helped spur them on. In the 1950s and early 1960s, many wineries that had produced wine in bulk to sell to other wineries began proudly labeling their wines under their own names and going public. At the same time, new young winemakers with their own ideas were enriching the mix. What one can only think of as a rush to excellence was on in earnest, and it continues.

II. What Is It?

There are several classes of wine: Appetizer and dessert wines, which include dry Sherries and sweet Sherries and Port; sparkling wines; pop wines and fruit wines; flavored wines, such as Vermouth; and table wines.

This book covers table wines — grape wines of between ten and fourteen percent alcohol, made in most cases to go with food, made in just about every country in the world with a temperate climate zone.

Many countries in Europe take a geographical approach to wine labeling and nomenclature. In California they take two approaches, the generic and the varietal.

Generic wines are blends of the juice of different grapes, with names tacked on by the European immigrants who tried to give an indication of the basic type of wine it was. Thus we have Chablis, Burgundy, Claret, etc. They don't resemble those wines of France, but winemakers have been stuck with them for years, as part of the fallout of the post-Prohibition ignorance. Today, more people are calling for "a glass of wine," and more labels reflect this; they say "white table wine" or "Sonoma Red."

Varietal wines are a different matter; they are named for the grape variety that predominates in the wine. Thus we have Pinot Noir, Chardonnay, etc.

This is as good a place as any to discuss one of the snobs' favorite complaints, and that is blending. They say that California wines are blended, and that makes them inferior. This is not only wrong, but stupid.

In the first place, many Europeans blend, and I am talking about French and Italian wines that can cost over twenty dollars a bottle and bear famous names. Cabernet Sauvignon is softened with some Merlot and other grapes to make fine Bordeaux, for example. Blending is simply something you do to improve the wine, unless you are unscrupulous and want to stretch the wine and improve your profits; the evidence, however, usually resides in the glass accusingly.

In the second place, there are a great many people in California who do not blend at all; sometimes the wines are too powerful as a result, but often not.

At any rate, the whole issue is usually a straw man; there is no reason to bring it up as a generalization. It is usually a sign of ignorance.

Are varietal wines better? Usually they cost more, but they are not a guarantee of quality. The name of the winery, your own budget and taste (and I hope this book) will determine the guidelines.

The question of pairing wine and food comes up a lot, because people seem to think that there is only one "right" wine to go with one dish. Others stick strictly to the red-with-meat, white-with-fish approach. Throughout the book, I've made a number of broad suggestions for all sorts of pairings, but the main thing to remember is that there is no exclusively right dish-and-wine combination.

On the other hand, it really is folly to drink a light, slightly sweet wine with a prime rib of beef — you wouldn't be doing either (let alone yourself) any justice; the rich flavors of each would just cancel each other out.

The basic thing to keep in mind is flavor types and especially intensities. If baked chicken is a five on a flavor scale of one to ten, then Chardonnay, which in most cases would rate an eight, is too strong; Riesling, with its delicacy, is probably a five, and the best match. Baking the chicken in a tomato sauce would probably raise it to a seven or eight and that, combined with the type of taste, would make it a good match with Gamay Beaujolais or Zinfandel. Shellfish, with their pronounced flavors, are up in the seven-to-eight range, and therefore merit a match with Chardonnay. And if you happen to make a meat-loaf that demands the time and effort to raise to a powerhouse ten, by all means have Cabernet Sauvignon with it — if you can make a meatloaf that earns a ten, you deserve it anyway.

Some of the wines mentioned in this book need some aging. This does not mean you have to dig up your back yard to start a cellar, or rent a vault somewhere. Wine can be safely stored in a closet, as long as it's away from heat, light and vibration, for a couple of years. Ideal temperature is fifty-five degrees, but at higher temperatures, up to seventy, it just ages faster.

Over that temperature, or in a prolonged hot spell, the wine can go bad. But wine isn't as fragile as people think, and it's worth taking a chance on if you're not in an area of climatic extremes.

III. What's That You Say?

The language of wine is basically simple, but in the hands of rhapsodizers lost in its heady delights, it has often gotten rather weird. It really does not demand that someone make a speech about it, or knock off a lyric ode. It is quite worth thinking about and savoring, but there is no need for anyone to feel defensive if he or she doesn't want to talk about it; like a lot of other pleasures in life, it can be shared but doesn't have to be advertised.

Here is a glossary of a few terms that are helpful in assessing wine, and using this book.

Aroma: This is simply the way the wine smells. There are different aromas present as the wine progresses, such as fermentation aroma, and at some point, to professionals, aroma becomes bouquet; it is a minor distinction that has caused more confusion and trouble than it's worth, at least for laymen. Some grape varieties have pronounced aroma.

Aroma is important because it can tell you more about the wine than taste — your nose is more sensitive than your tongue. You should only fill a wine glass halfway, leaving room in it for the aroma to develop increasing your enjoyment of the wine.

Acid: Acidity in wine can be good or bad, depending on the type and amount. When the right amount is present, it gives the wine a fresh and pleasant tartness, a little bite, in the same way that oranges and apples have.

Sugar: Grapes and wines contain fructose and glucose, two fruit sugars. The sugar should balance the acid to produce a pleasant taste; too much sugar and not enough acid, and you have a "flabby" wine (just as you have the flabby abomination, the Golden Delicious apple). On the other hand, a wine with too much acid will be disagreeably sharp.

Dry wines usually contain less than one-and-a-half percent sugar by the time they finish fermenting.

Fruity: The term describes a fresh, tart, pleasant fruit-like impression, and is a hallmark of a well-made wine. A wine not so well made would seem flat, not fresh.

Body: Basically, this refers to the feel of the wine in the mouth, related to alcohol and viscosity. A light-bodied wine would probably be unbalanced; most wines are medium-bodied, a few are heavy-bodied.

Astringency: This comes from tannins in the wine, and gives a puckery impression on the tongue; tannins are the same substances that give tea its puckery quality. It helps wine to be long-lived and smooths out with age.

Finish: The impression left in your mouth after you swallow: the aftertaste. With most table wines it should be refreshing, clean and the flavor should linger.

IV. Wine and Health

Wine, in moderation of course, is good for you. Mainly, it goes with food in a variety of ways — gets the juices flowing in your mouth and stomach, makes the food taste better, and aids your digestion. It contains just under twenty-five calories an ounce, so you don't have to give it up when you diet. It contains some vitamins and minerals.

It also contains alcohol, of course, and that gives some people fits; I can only say that, as a wine-drinker, I'm usually the one who gets to drive other people home after parties.

V. About This Book

There are several criteria I used in compiling this book, and it's only fair that you should be aware of them.

There are a great many marvelous wines made in such small amounts that none of us will ever see them; I may have heard of them, but without first-hand knowledge, couldn't in all conscience include them. I have, however, included some that may be hard to find but worth the search.

In some categories, such as Chardonnay and Cabernet Sauvignon, where California is busting out all over with excellence, the choices were many and difficult, complicated by the fact that there are wines in those categories which are not prime thoroughbreds, but offer excellent value. As this is intended to be a consumer guide, I have touched on as many of those wines as possible.

There are many new wineries in California making excellent wine which have not established a track record yet; thus winery X may have made a legendary Zinfandel in 1974, but an indifferent one in 1975. Another may have won a gold medal someplace for its first vintage, which was last year. Consistency in at least three vintages became part of my equation; the brilliant newcomers will, I'm sure, find a place in future editions.

Finally, I hope you find this book enjoyable as well as useful. It's not definitive, nothing dealing with California wine and all its excitement and ferment can be; think of it as your launching platform.

Many colleges and community centers offer courses in wine, and may be a good place to check out for further exploration of the world of wine. However, there is no way of knowing about the quality of the instruction; if the class includes tastings, you will at least have that opportunity to sample and thus learn under your own hat, so to speak.

There are two good groups with many chapters in California, and around the country, which conduct many tastings (which is, after all, the best way to learn). They frequently feature well-qualified speakers, too, as well as dinners and excursions.

One is WINO, an abominable name which stands for "Wine Instruction for Novices and Oenophiles;" it is at 13910 La Jolla Plaza, Garden Grove, CA 92640. Write, and they'll tell you if there is a chapter near you.

The other is Les Amis du Vin; the West Coast headquarters is at P.O. Box 49424, Los Angeles, CA 90049. The National headquarters is at 2302 Perkins Place, Silver Spring, MD 20910. Both of these groups are highly recommended.

ABOUT THE AUTHOR

Alexander Mackenzie is a pseudonym. The author worked in the restaurant trade in Boston, New York, and Baltimore, acquiring a knowledge and appreciation of fine wines as he rose through the ranks. He was associated with a wine importer in New York before moving to Southern California, where he became a restaurant consultant and wine buyer. He is a member of the International Wine and Food Society, a Chevalier du Tastevin and several other wine and food societies.

THE BEST
RED WINES
OF CALIFORNIA

THE TOP 10
CABERNET SAUVIGNONS

For those who have worked their way up the wine ladder, the Cabernet Sauvignon grape sits comfortably and easily at the top. It makes the great wines of Bordeaux, and the great wines of California, which I think, at their best, are equal to the Bordeaux.

Good Cabernet is almost never cheap, and should never be drunk young — five years is the minimum (and that's having it in its adolescence); at ten years it should be just hitting its stride, at fifteen or even twenty it should be perfect.

But what to do in the meantime, or if one doesn't have a cellar? One recourse is to try Louis Martini's Cabernet, which sells for under four dollars, and is a very good wine; it tastes like Cabernet ought to taste and is usually ready to drink when it's on the market. In good years, which is most of the time, it may even be aged a while, and usually surprises people by aging gracefully longer then expected. Why isn't it on the list? Because it lacks the complexity and elegance of the wineries listed; it aspires only to be very good and not great. Try it and see; you'll thank Mr. Martini for the price as well as the value received.

From time to time, under odd names, other Cabernets are released at low prices, usually bought by enterprising merchants from wineries needing fast cash. Some excellent values can be found under the Round Hill label, from Lost Hills, and from second labels of established wineries. Ask the clerk at a good store that does a lot of wine business any time you see a Cabernet that is under five dollars; at that price, it's worth trying a bottle.

The flavors of Cabernet Sauvignon, as befits such a classic wine, are complex; tannins give it a puckery, astringent quality like strong tea. Some find it herbaceous, similar perhaps to dried basil; there is also a pleasantly vegetative undertone reminiscent of fresh green peppers. And in California, at least, there is frequently a minty, eucalyptus quality to the aroma and taste.

These are all somewhat clumsy attempts to define a fleeting set of impressions that, in the best Cabernets, come together in the aroma and on the palate. When they are all in balance, with good acid and fruitiness and a touch of oak, nothing stands out, but there are enough different notes resounding for a symphony. And age, pulling them all together, softening the tone, is the concertmaster.

Other quite respectable Cabernets at under five dollars: Pedroncelli, San Martin, Sebastiani, Sonoma Vineyards, and Souverain of Alexander Valley.

Cabernet Sauvignon goes well with any meat, but best with full-flavored ones, like roast beef or lamb.

BURGESS CELLARS. This small Napa winery, perched atop a mountain, turns out some rather elegant red wines. The 1974 and 1975 Cabernets, at under eight dollars, are among them — medium-bodied, moderately tannic, with an appealing fruitiness underlying the flavors. A couple of years in the bottle are warranted. The 1974 Vintage Selection, at twelve dollars, is a twenty-year wine of great character.

CLOS DU VAL. This Napa winery has only been around for a short time, but the wines (just Cabernet and Zinfandel) have been excellent from the start. The owner-winemaker is Bernard Portet, a Frenchman who grew up in the wine business and obviously paid attention. The 1974 vintage is a typical full-bodied claret in the California style — hints of mint and oak in the aroma, with a ripeness of fruit and some astringency in the flavor. Another one to lay away for a long time; nine dollars.

HEITZ WINE CELLARS. It's perhaps indicative of the boom in California wine that this grand-daddy of California Cabernet makers is less than twenty years old — the winery, not Joe Heitz. Good wine starts with good grapes, and Heitz knows how to choose them. His "Martha's Vineyard" selections are invariably expensive and also great; the 1972 and 1973 are currently available at fifteen and thirteen dollars. In the meantime, while one waits for them to come around, there is the regular bottling of 1973's vintage at under seven dollars, and it is "regular" only by comparison to the Martha's Vineyard wines — generous and full, it is a bargain.

MAYACAMAS VINEYARDS. Another small mountaintop winery in Napa, noted for big and powerful wines. The 1973, at nine dollars, is a little softer than usual, but quite elegant and full of fruit. It will be another five years before it's ready, but well worth the wait.

ROBERT MONDAVI WINERY. The 1974 Cabernet is one of the most widely available and will be ready to drink in a year or two (even now if you like tannins). At eight dollars, it's quite reasonable. The only problem may be that the word is getting out about its elegant charms, so you'll have to move fast. There is also a 1973 "Reserve" at fifteen dollars.

PARDUCCI WINE CELLARS. Now here is a simple, honest Cabernet that is also less than five dollars for the 1973 and 1974 — excellent values. They lack some of the complexity of the others, but have a nice tart, astringent flavor. A bit of time in the bottle would smooth out the slightly rough edges of the 1974, though the 1973 is fine now.

RIDGE VINEYARDS. Ridge is noted for big powerhouse wines with lots of oak, and the 1974 "Monte Bello" (ten dollars) is no exception. It'll just hit its stride in 1980. Good flavors once you get past the oak, with a black-currant ripeness predominating, and moderate tannins.

SIMI WINERY. This is a nice, unpretentious wine, pleasantly soft, but with nice full flavor and an easy price — six dollars. The aroma hints of violets, and the aftertaste is clean and refreshing.

SPRING MOUNTAIN VINEYARDS. Another characteristic of California Cabernets is a note in the aroma akin to cedar — very pleasant, and this winery's 1975 has it. There is mint at the edges of its very fruity taste, and the finish is astringent and tart. An elegant, excellent wine; under nine dollars.

STAG'S LEAP WINE CELLARS. Probably the hottest Cabernet around after its victory in the Paris tasting a while back, when it beat out several famous Bordeaux — with French tasters, yet. That was the 1973; the 1974 was even better, and the 1975, quite good, is on the market today. Its posted price is $8.50, and if your retailer is selling it for that, he's a saint — I've seen it for twelve. It's a sleek and supple wine that should age for four or five years at least.

THE TOP 10
PINOT NOIRS

Pinot Noir is a tricky, difficult grape to make into good wine, and it isn't helped by comparisons people make to the great French Burgundies, like Chambertin. What those people tend to overlook, however, is that eight out of ten times, French red Burgundies aren't too hot any more.

The same restless tinkering going on with other California wines is going on with Pinot Noir, however, and they've gotten better — several are quite good, and they'll be joined by others in years to come.

Ideally, Pinot Noir is soft, even velvety in texture, with a pleasant fullness and slight, almost peppermint, tang in the flavor. California Pinot Noirs, perhaps because of the slightly warmer climate, tend not to be too acid. The consensus is that they are best at three or four years old, but I've had them ten years old and marvelous, showing at that age some kinship to their French cousins.

This is one wine where the vintage date matters a bit more than the others for us average palates; most recent years have been quite good, so that the winemaker had the maximum to work with in most areas. In 1977, it was a trifle cool for the maximum ripening most prefer, and it will take all the skill they possess to make excellent Pinot Noir. The people listed have shown they have it, so they're still a good bet for 1977 — and beyond.

CHALONE VINEYARDS. Easily the best Pinot Noir in California or darn near anyplace else, year in and year out — a full-bodied, rich, long-lived wine, hand-made in the Burgundy style. Dark-red, oaky and big, it's hard to find in stores, even with its deserved ten-dollar pricetag. The 1973 and 1974 versions are available, and should be tucked away for four or five years to mellow into something fantastic.

HANZELL VINEYARDS. This Sonoma winery makes just two wines, both Burgundy classics — Pinot Noir and Chardonnay. The Pinot Noir is aged in French oak, also hand-made, and hard to find but worth the search. Velvety, almost chocolaty in texture, with a floral/minty aroma, it too needs a few years to come around to ambrosia. The 1972 and 1973 vintages are what to look for. And make a note to look for the 1974 next year, the 1975 the year after, and so on. . . Only eight dollars.

LLORDS & ELWOOD. The testimony at hand is a non-vintage, with a label strip noting that it was bottled in Autumn 1976; perhaps it's from the excellent 1974 vintage, with some other wine blended in from an earlier vintage. Certainly it has a pleasant aroma suggesting proper bottle-aging, a creamy texture and rich flavor, and a clean, almost sweet finish. Hard to find, a bargain at under five dollars, and considering the good 1975 vintage for this variety, maybe they'll do it this well again.

LOUIS MARTINI WINERY. The 1974 out now is an excellent example of a medium-bodied classic California Pinot Noir — fairly fruity, flavorful and velvety in the mouth. Very pleasant wine, and under four dollars too.

ROBERT MONDAVI WINERY. One of the consistent successes of this consistently successful winery is Pinot Noir. French oak is part of it, but dedication and skill are a bigger part. The 1973 and 1974 are available now, and in good supply, and nicely priced at just over five dollars. The wine has elegance and balance, medium body and a perfect smack of varietal flavor. Very tasty now, and will be even better in a year or two, although you'd better buy it now if you want to have it then.

MOUNT EDEN VINEYARDS. Like the Chalone, from grapes grown on an arid mountaintop, made by hand in small lots, and highly distinctive, requiring several years of bottle age to mellow out. Assertive, full-bodied, peppery and tannic, but lots of fruit underneath which will come forward with time. The 1973 is under eight dollars, the 1974 around ten.

JOSEPH PHELPS VINEYARDS. The 1973 and 1974 versions are a little lighter in color and body than some of the others, but no less attractive wines. Moderately soft, ready to drink now, they are lively wines and a bargain at under five dollars.

SAN MARTIN VINEYARDS. The grapes came from Monterey, but the excellent character of the wine had to come from the talent of the winemaker, who coaxed a lot of flavor out of them. At under four dollars, an exceptional value. The 1974 is ready to drink now, medium-bodied, mellow and full of flavor.

STERLING VINEYARDS. An odd wine, dark and rough, with a slightly alcoholic bite in the aftertaste. Still, it has a richness of flavor that promises some rewards with aging. The 1974 has the edge over the 1973; both are around six dollars.

Z-D WINES. This tiny Sonoma winery makes wines in individual small lots from different vineyards, and so labels them. Some are better than others, but all are good. They are sturdy wines that ideally should be cellared for a couple of years to reach full potential. The color is deep ruby, the aroma is complex, almost herbal, and the body is full. The taste of the 1973's and 1974's is a little harsh yet, but complex and fruity, with strong hints of oak and tannin. Around seven dollars.

THE TOP 10
LIGHT ZINFANDELS

The origins of Zinfandel are obscure, and this has led to its becoming known as California's mystery grape. Most of the stories about its beginnings are romantic, but it succeeded because it was a good workhorse grape, and made tart and tasty wines in a variety of styles. While it was never a sow's ear, it certainly has been a silk purse in the hands of some talented winemakers.

Current thinking at UC Davis is that it is actually the Primitivo grape of Italy, though it yields a different and much better wine in California. Like the hero of many romantic novels about Knights of the Round Table, it was mis-identified from the start, and only after much tribulation emerged into glory.

One of California's most popular grapes, it grows from Mendocino to Riverside County. Over 100 wineries make Zinfandel in a variety of styles. One group favors the light and fruity, ready-to-drink-now approach; another aims for dark, heavy and tannic wines worthy of cellaring; and there is a group that makes them full-bodied, with a hint of sweetness — known as "country wines."

Zinfandel was characterized, not entirely accurately, as the American Beaujolais for a long time. It does have a similar light and fresh quality, but it is much more tart than Beaujolais, and generally ages better than most of them.

The flavor is characterized as reminiscent of blackberries, also distinct in the aroma; it is a wine that is very easy to like.

The most useful way to approach Zinfandel, it seems to me, is to separate it into two categories: the light and fruity ones, and the heavy, tannic, claret-styled ones. There is usually a few dollars difference in the price, reflecting the extra cellar treatment, time in oak, etc. of the ambitious ones, and vintages tend to matter less in the light versions, though I've cited what's on the market as we go to press.

As a generalization, it seems safe to say that if it's under four dollars, it's ready to drink now. Of all the categories in this book, this light Zinfandel one was one of the most difficult, because there are so many pleasant wines. It also seems safe to say that, whether you are a novice or connoisseur, there are several Zinfandels for you, probably quite a few.

BANDIERA WINERY. This Sonoma winery has been around for over forty years, but has just recently been reorganized and revitalized. If they continue in the same vein as this 1974 Zinfandel, they'll do fine. It's medium-bodied, with a ripe, fresh taste and a tart, astringent finish. Three dollars.

CHRISTIAN BROTHERS. One of the most reliable Zinfandels in California. Non-vintaged, it is light and fresh, with good acid underlying the full flavor. Three dollars.

CRESTA BLANCA WINERY. From Mendocino, a non-vintage bargain (under three dollars). Full fruit flavors and some spiciness with a hint of wood underneath; nice aftertaste.

GUNDLACH-BUNDSCHU WINERY. This Sonoma winery started 120 years ago and had a lot of starts and stops along the way to its current success. The 1973 and 1974 Zinfandels are quite good proof that they're probably going to be around a long time. The wines have good, intense color, complex aroma, and flavor (oak, tannin, fruit, acid) in abundance. Lots of character for just under four dollars.

KENWOOD VINEYARDS. More variable than some others on this list; in good years, they sometimes try for a big Zinfandel. However they go, the results are usually excellent. The 1975 is medium-bodied with good fruit and some tannin and oak to reinforce it. A sturdier wine than the others, it's more of an intermediate Zinfandel, but no less charming for that. Four dollars.

CHARLES KRUG WINERY. This is a rather dependable middle-of-the-road Zinfandel that should not be overlooked. Somewhat soft in its first impression, it has enough body and tannin to follow through nicely, and the price is nice too — three dollars.

LOUIS MARTINI WINERY. Of all these bargains, this may be the best. Under three dollars, it has a lovely aroma of wild berries, medium body and plenty of fruit and just the right smack of tartness. Smooth, fruity finish. The 1974 version is a perfect example.

SEBASTIANI WINERY. The major contender, with Martini, for the long-running, low-priced Zinfandel success year in and year out. Full and spicy, dark and quite fruity, it has a clean aftertaste. Under three dollars.

SIMI WINERY. This is an excellent wine from Sonoma, medium bodied, with light and lively flavors, some wood hints in the taste, nice acid and astringency. A trifle overpriced at under five dollars.

SONOMA VINEYARDS. For under three dollars, this is an excellent everyday wine. The aroma is clean and berryish, the flavor tart and astringent, with the fruit peeking through. Quite likeable.

Fans of these big, powerhouse wines often say that they should be laid down and forgotten for ten years at least, but I'm not so sure. I've found that the full balance of flavor seems to occur when they are from five to seven years old; any more than that, and the fruit flavors may fade. In general, my philosophy is, better a little sooner than too late.

You may occasionally see a Zinfandel costing eight dollars or more labeled "Late Harvest" or "Essence." These wines are usually from grapes left on the vine till the last possible minute, and picked at high sugar levels. The resulting wine often comes out at fifteen or sixteen percent alcohol, and still usually has some perceptible sweetness. The wines are pleasant oddities, but they are not table wines, meant to go with a meal; they can be aged for several years, and then consumed, like Port, after a meal. On the other hand, you can get an excellent Port, like Ficklin or J. W. Morris, for less money and have a better wine.

The light Zinfandels are good and amiable companions for all meats. The heavy ones that follow should probably be reserved for fuller-flavored dishes, such as leg of lamb or prime rib.

BURGESS CELLARS. This is one of the lighter heavy Zinfandels, needing only another year or so to fully come together in the bottle, though it could even be consumed now if you don't mind some astringency from the tannins. The 1974 is a shade lighter than the 1975, though they share a harmonious style. Soft but full-flavored, with a touch of oak, it's a bargain at just over five dollars.

CARNEROS CREEK. This winery has made some fine wines in several types, and their 1975 is one of them, nicely priced at under four dollars. It's not big, but is rather oaky, and would need two or three years to smooth out. Otherwise, it has a good fruity flavor and tart, astringent finish.

CLOS DU VAL. An excellent wine, dark, tannic, with a spicy aroma, berry flavors and pleasant acidity. Both the 1973 and 1974 should be consumed when five or six years old. At under five dollars, the 1973 was a bargain, but the price for the 1974 jumped to over seven dollars, which is a little overpriced.

MAYACAMAS VINEYARD. Bob Travers makes big and oaky wines that do take several years to smooth out, and this is one of them. They also sell like hotcakes, so if you see one, and are looking for a big wine, grab it. The 1973, at six dollars, was a rich and interesting wine, just a bit low in fruit; the 1974 is much more balanced, a rich and beautiful wine.

ROBERT MONDAVI WINERY. One of the more complex Zinfandels, this one combines fruit, tannin, oak and acidity very well; nice astringent finish. The 1974 and 1975 could be consumed now or held a little while. Ambitious wine, and it succeeds.

CHATEAU MONTELENA. This is a lively wine, medium-bodied but feeling heavier than it is due to a good balance of fruit, acid and oak. The 1974 version is around now, and worth looking for; just over five dollars.

MONTEVINA. This small winery in Amador County makes a couple of different Zinfandels, all from old vines and fairly heavy. The regular bottling is under five dollars, and a rich, full dark, wine. The lighter style, designated "Montino," is somehow intense and soft at the same time, and sells for less than four dollars.

RIDGE VINEYARDS. This winery makes Zinfandels from several individual vineyards, and so designates them on the label; thus, we have the "Geyserville," "Shenandoah," "Fiddletown," "Lytton Springs," "Monte Bello," and so on, depending where they purchased the grapes. They average in price from five to six dollars, and I have to admire them for lowering the prices in some years that are not as good as others. The house style which links these wines calls for plenty of color, tannins, oak and fairly high alcohol (around thirteen percent). Though Ridge wines are noted for heaviness, I've noticed that they seem to have been getting lighter lately. The side labels are mini-encyclopedias on the wines, and will tell you all you need to know about them — or perhaps even more. Ridge also makes a blended Zinfandel, called "Coast Range," for under four dollars, meant to be consumed over the short run, while you wait for the others to mature.

SUTTER HOME. This winery specializes in Zinfandel; it's all they make, including a white version. The 1974 shows them hitting their stride — it's a big, rough wine, dark and tannic, and needs aging very much, perhaps another two years at least. Just over four dollars.

JOSEPH SWAN. One of the most controversial winemakers in California is Joseph Swan; his wines are distinctive and quite unique, there are never large amounts available, and they sell out quickly. They are usually rich, complex and intense wines, and prices vary from five dollars to what a retailer thinks he can get away with charging. If you see a bottle, it's probably worth trying; you may be the only kid on your block — or even your city — to have tried Joseph Swan Zinfandel. And you might even like it.

THE TOP 10
PETITE SIRAHS

Petite Sirah, like a few other California grapes, has a tangled and uncertain ancestry. Once thought to be the classic Rhone grape that produces the fine Hermitage wines and is part of the blend of Chateauneuf-du-Pape, it's now suspected of being the less-than-noble Duriff.

There are people who spend a lot of time worrying about this sort of thing instead of thinking about the pleasures of what's in the bottle, but after you try these ten, you probably won't be one of them.

Petite Sirah was frequently used as a blending wine, partly because of its deep color, partly because it added acidity and an intriguing grace note of flavor. A little over ten years ago Concannon started bottling it as a varietal, and soon others followed suit. As the rush to excellence started in the late Sixties-early Seventies, this wine came into its own more and more.

Today's Petite Sirahs are generally dark, inky and rather tannic, full-bodied, with a delightfully mild spicy edge to their flavor. It's a wine that demands great care if it's to come out well, so it's no surprise that the best examples come from small wineries that can take the time to make the effort.

These wines ought to be laid down for a while to smooth out; I've indicated which are closest to being ready now. Match them with the most flavored meats.

BURGESS CELLARS. Both the 1973 and 1974 vintages of this small Napa Valley winery are superb, everything a Petite Sirah ought to be. Around five dollars.

CONCANNON VINEYARDS. Some connoisseurs put down this wine because it's made in a lighter, ready-to-drink-now style, but if you don't have a cellar it's a good choice. Both the 1973 and the 1974 vintages are quite pleasant. Around four dollars.

FREEMARK ABBEY. This winery is noted for other wines, but with the 1974 they've gotten themselves a winner — dark and intense in flavor, complex, so full-bodied you can almost chew on it. Put some of this in a closet and try to forget about it for a couple of years — you'll be well rewarded. Around five dollars.

ROBERT MONDAVI WINERY. This may be one of Mondavi's best wines, which is saying a lot. The 1973 and 1974 have everything going for them that a Petite Sirah ought to, and a smooth and almost silky texture going through your mouth on top of that. The 1973 is almost gone. Around five dollars.

PARDUCCI WINE CELLARS. Up in Mendocino, the Parducci family makes a lot of good wine, and this is one of their best. The 1972 and 1973 are not only good, but quite a bargain at under four dollars; ready to drink now, too. Given the good harvest conditions of 1974, theirs will undoubtedly be the best of the bunch, but don't wait — savor the '72 and '73 till it comes out.

RIDGE VINEYARDS. This Santa Clara winery has a reputation for making big, bold wines, and their Petite Sirahs uphold it. The 1973, 1974 and 1975 vintages are available, though you might have to hunt for them. They do require aging, but the 1975 is a little lighter. Around six dollars.

SONOMA VINEYARDS. This wine is in a slightly different style than the others, but no less interesting. Dark, tannic, full bodied and a definite bargain at three dollars..

SOUVERAIN OF ALEXANDER VALLEY. The 1974 is on the market right now, and it's quite a bargain at three dollars. Not as assertive as the others, it's a very pleasant wine with a nice fruity taste, clean and astringent.

STAG'S LEAP VINEYARD. This is not the winery that won the Paris tasting, but another that shares a similar — and disputed — name. The 1973 and 1974 are terrific, full of varietal character, like velvet in the mouth, yet not so powerful that you have to cellar them for years. They're hard to find due to a small supply, despite the slightly overpriced seven-dollar tag.

STONEGATE WINERY. Perhaps the best of the bunch, the 1974 and 1975 vintages are just outstanding. They're not as heavy as some of the others but still have an almost overpowering fruity flavor — almost like biting into a bunch of fresh grapes; the aroma fairly jumps out of the glass at you. Around six dollars, hard to find, worth the money and search.

THE TOP 10 GAMAYS/GAMAY BEAUJOLAIS

There are some semantic antics going on with these wines, a result of some honest confusion. Gamay is the "true" grape of the Beaujolais region of France; Gamay Beaujolais is actually a clone of Pinot Noir that was mis-identified quite a few years ago. People who like to fuss about such things are free to do so, while the rest of us simply enjoy the light and agreeable wines both grapes produce.

The fact of the matter is that before anyone knew of the differences, both grapes were vinified in a light style, similar to Beaujolais wines. They are meant to be consumed quite young, compensating for their relative lack of complexity with freshness and fruitiness.

Some of the wines listed below are vintage-dated, and some are not; the only reason for paying attention to dates here is that you want them young, less than three years old, before their somewhat fragile charms have faded.

Gamays and Gamay Beaujolais go well with light red meats, and even chicken on a winter night.

As we were going to press with this book, San Martin released a Soft Gamay Beaujolais, containing just over ten percent alcohol. I didn't taste it, so can't include it, but if all I have heard about it is true, it's light and fruity and worth seeking out.

BEAULIEU VINEYARDS. This Gamay Beaujolais is a little deeper and richer than some of the others, with a slight zingy sharpness. Just over three dollars.

CHRISTIAN BROTHERS. The Gamay Noir is the "true" Gamay grape, with some older wine blended in for softness. At under four dollars, it is an agreeable and mellow quaff. The Brothers also make a Gamay Beaujolais, also nice.

DRY CREEK. This Gamay Beaujolais is a trifle more ambitious than the others, a little more tannic and full-bodied. It could even age a little bit. Just over three dollars.

KENWOOD VINEYARDS. A light and tart Gamay Beaujolais from Sonoma, this one shows a closer affinity some years to its Pinot Noir progenitor, which can make it a bargain at under three dollars.

MIRASSOU VINEYARDS. This Gamay Beaujolais is a blend of grapes from Santa Clara Valley and Monterey, though the emphasis is tending toward Monterey as those vines mature. A very dark wine for the type, medium-bodied and dry. Under four dollars.

ROBERT MONDAVI WINERY. This one's a Gamay, and in many ways reminiscent of a French Beaujolais — and a good one at that. The fresh fruitiness of the wine could almost pass for a bit of sweetness; it is most engaging, just over three dollars.

MONTEREY VINEYARDS. Another Gamay Beaujolais from Monterey County, very fresh and appealing, with a light garnet color and light, lively taste. Three dollars.

PARDUCCI WINE CELLARS. From Mendocino, this Gamay Beaujolais may benefit from the cooler climate, which enables it to ripen slower; or maybe it's the Parducci talent. Whatever, this is quite a sturdy and straightforward version of the variety. Three dollars.

SEBASTIANI VINEYARDS. This is one of the most consistently fresh and appealing Gamay Beaujolais made in California; they must have access to good vineyards. Clean and fresh, slightly tart, it's a delight. Just over three dollars.

STAG'S LEAP WINE CELLARS. For a Gamay Beaujolais, this is a rather serious wine — a little ponderous. The flavors are good, the price is right (under four dollars), it's just not quite as lively as the others; withal, a good bottle of wine.

Among the odd lots of lesser-known wine types are found some very intriguing ones. Some, like Grignolino and Charbono, are simply made in small amounts. Barbera, on the other hand, is widely available but mostly in jug blends or overly sweet, heavy wines. At any rate, they shouldn't be overlooked just because they've never had the chance to become fashionable.

MARTINI Barbera. An Italian grape, Barbera produces a somewhat rough wine that goes quite well with Italian foods. It's dark and possesses good acid and robust flavor, quite dry. Although it arrives at the marketplace ready to drink, it can age rather gracefully for a few years. Under four dollars.

SEBASTIANI Barbera. This version is a little lighter than Martini's, and usually smoother and fruitier, while having similar attributes on color and acidity. Under four dollars.

FORTINO Charbono. Another Italian grape, yielding a softer wine than Barbera, though somewhat similar. Fortino makes it into a full-bodied wine, with a barely perceptible touch of sweetness. The wine was hard to find, but since winning a Gold Medal at the Los Angeles County Fair, may be more widely available. It's under four dollars.

INGLENOOK Charbono. For a long while, Inglenook was the only winery making Charbono, and their experience shows. It has some finesse in good years, though at over four dollars it's a trifle overpriced.

SEBASTIANI Nouveau. Every year, about mid-November, the Sebastianis release a Gamay Beaujolais from that harvest — about six weeks old. It's lightly fermented and meant to be consumed immediately; its flavors are less of Gamay Beaujolais than sheer exuberant grapiness. Under four dollars.

HEITZ Grignolino. Yet another Italian grape, and quite an unusual wine — light in color, with an orange tint, quite tart and astringent, even spicy. Goes well with Italian foods and especially ham. Under four dollars.

BERINGER Grignolino. A slightly subdued version of the Heitz style, but no less appealing. Darker, with less of an orange tint, it is a brisk and bracing wine. Under four dollars.

CHRISTIAN BROTHERS Pinot St. George. This grape is so far unique to the Christian Brothers; it makes a complex and elegant wine, a little light but well rounded, with a character all its own. Under five dollars.

MONTEVINA Zinfandel Nuevo. Like the Sebastiani Nouveau, this wine is released after light fermentation, usually only a few months after the harvest, and meant to be consumed right away. Light, lively, fruity. Around four dollars.

STERLING VINEYARDS Merlot. Perhaps the best of an up-and-coming variety in California; Merlot is used to soften Cabernet Sauvignon in various Bordeaux blends, and on its own is a delightfully opulent, supple wine, at least in this version. It is a bit overpriced at around seven dollars, but worth a try.

THE TOP 10
JUG REDS

Jug wines used to be simple half-gallons and gallons of generic wines, like California Burgundy, made in a hearty style with a touch of sweetness, perfect companions to meatloaf or backyard barbeques. But the wines they are a-changing, and so are the sizes. Thanks to the government, wine is going metric, and the old gallons and half-gallons are giving way to one-and-a-half liter and three-liter sizes. The former contains fifty-one ounces, the latter 102 — equal, in other words, to two or four fifth-size bottles. The whole industry will be metric soon, so you might as well learn the new sizes.

The other change is due to two forces: Consumers who grew increasingly sophisticated about wine, which is to say wanted the stuff drier, and to August Sebastiani, who decided to bottle varietals (Cabernet Sauvignon, Chardonnay and Pinot Noir) in gallons and half-gallons. Now it's quite common, and we are better for it. Thank you, Gus.

The one-and-a-half-liter size is also known as a magnum, and that's the nomenclature I've adopted. It should also be pointed out that the larger the size, the larger the saving. Thus, a half-gallon might cost $3.49, while a gallon of the same wine will cost $5.99. Most wines will keep perfectly well, if stored in the refrigerator, for up to a week. A good trick is to transfer unused wine into smaller bottles, limiting the wine's contact with air, thus increasing its ability to retain flavor.

FOPPIANO VINEYARDS Zinfandel. Robust and appealing wine, with a little depth of character and complexity. Under three dollars for a magnum.

GALLO Hearty Burgundy. People who started out with this wine (and there are a lot of us), have noticed that the taste has changed a little over the years. It seems to be a little lighter, and also a little fruitier. It's under three dollars for a magnum.

GALLO Barbera. A little heartier and a little drier than Gallo's Hearty Burgundy, and a good buy at just over three dollars for a magnum.

KENWOOD VINEYARDS Burgundy. The side label tells you that the wine is mostly Pinot Noir, with Cabernet, Zinfandel and a few other varieties tossed in, making a sturdy wine with interesting complexity and flavor. Above average, and just under three dollars for a magnum.

LOUIS MARTINI WINERY Mountain Red. This wine is not only dry and hearty, it has a touch of tartness that is very appealing. Over three dollars for a magnum.

CK MONDAVI Zinfandel. This is one of the wines that has grown perceptibly drier over the years. It is now a fresh and pleasant wine, light but lively. A bargain at over three dollars a half-gallon.

ROBERT MONDAVI WINERY Red Table Wine. This wine is a blend of several varieties, and is quite well-made; it has some complexity and depth of character, and is a good everyday wine to go with meals. Under four dollars for a magnum.

PEDRONCELLI WINERY Sonoma Red. **One of the more** attractive and reliable jug reds for years has been this one, a sturdy rascal with plenty of flavor and a bit of tartness. At just over three dollars a half-gallon, a bargain.

SEBASTIANI WINERY Mountain Cabernet Sauvignon. The one that started it all remains one of the better ones, dry and full-flavored, with nice Cabernet astringency and a pleasant softness. Just under five dollars for a half-gallon.

SONOMA VINEYARDS Zinfandel. This wine is almost too classy to be called a "jug wine." Very nice Zinfandel aroma and flavor, with a touch of tannin and good depth of flavor. Over four dollars a magnum.

THE TOP
WHITE WINES
OF CALIFORNIA

THE TOP 10
CHARDONNAYS

Most people in the wine world agree that Chardonnay is easily California's biggest success story to date. Perhaps it is the growing conditions, perhaps it is the prod of knowing you are going up against some of the noblest wines of France, the White Burgundies that Dumas declared should be drunk kneeling with one's head bared.

Certainly, ambition must be a large part of it, because few people in California are trying to make a pleasant, middle-of-the-road wine; they are going for power and complexity, making wines that for the most part demand some aging to smooth out the flavors, especially oak.

There is some controversy over oak in Chardonnay in California, and it is merited. Sometimes oak is all you can taste in a few of these young monsters, and people wonder if there will be any fruit left when the oak fades to a proper vanillin grace note.

But most are in balance, and many achieve the greatness they aspire to. Along with that comes a fairly high price tag, and it is not uncommon to see them fetching eight, nine and even twelve dollars. Is it a fair price? Well, the better-known French White Burgundies are costing twice as much. And there are obviously plenty of people who will obviously shell out the money, as evidenced by the fact that the better-known California Chardonnays disappear from the shelves as fast as they are stocked. The recent drought, which reduced yields and drove grape prices up, didn't help matters at all.

Still, there are values, and I've tried to indicate some of them, along with a few notions of style in the wines at hand.

There is an admirable group of people who make the wine in a lighter style, frequently with little or no time in oak; less cellar treatment saves costs, and they pass some of the savings on to the consumer. Their character and charms may be a little lighter than the ones listed, but they are excellent values and a good introduction to what all the fuss is about. They are made by Parducci, Martini, Pedroncelli, Sebastiani, Wente, San Martin, and the Christian Brothers, and they are all under five dollars.

Incidentally, Chardonnay is also called Pinot Chardonnay, though it is not a member of that family. It's another long-ago error, and there is more and more of a trend to label it correctly.

The current vintage available, though not for long, is 1975; some 1976s are also coming out. The vintage is important for Chardonnay, as it does like a little age before it comes around. Four years old is a good age for sampling, five is usually better.

The flavor association most people make with Chardonnay is apples, and there is some resemblance to the crisp, fresh tartness of cold-climate apples like Macintoshes.

BURGESS CELLARS. Another powerhouse wine, slightly high in alcohol, with assertive oakiness. There's good varietal flavor lurking in there, too, however. Under nine dollars.

CHATEAU ST. JEAN. As usual with this winery, a potpourri of vineyard names and prices. Suffice it to say they're all quite elegant and authoritative examples. Most are just over seven dollars and worth it; others go up to twelve dollars, and don't necessarily have that much more richness of flavor.

FREEMARK ABBEY WINERY. Not as big as some of the others, but no less elegant — perfect combination of fruit, acid, oak and varietal character. Eight dollars.

HACIENDA WINE CELLARS. This is a nice light version of the variety, with especially nice aroma, good medium body and plenty of fruit in the flavor, with only a hint of oak. A bargain at less than seven dollars, but hard to find.

HANZELL VINEYARDS. This Sonoma winery really started the trend to French oak in Chardonnay, and continues to make ambitious and admirable wines, needing at least five years in the bottle and preferably a little more to come together. When it does, it's a delight. Hard to find, and worth the search. Nine dollars.

HEITZ CELLARS. A medium-bodied wine, with good acid and just a touch of oak, and excellent varietal flavor. Under ten dollars. Heitz also makes a non-vintage version that is a bargain at around five dollars.

MAYACAMAS VINEYARDS. Bob Travers makes power-houses, adding high alcohol to an already rich blend of acid, fruit and oak, but it helps the wine live a long time. Around eight dollars.

ROBERT MONDAVI WINERY. This is a sleek and elegant wine, bursting with fruitiness, possessed of nicely rounded varietal character. Lighter than the others, but a clear bargain at under seven dollars.

SPRING MOUNTAIN VINEYARDS. This winery has had a string of successes with Chardonnay, and this wine is another, though a little lighter than before. It's quite charming, with plenty of flavor and just a touch of oak. Nine dollars.

Z-D WINES. This Sonoma winery makes a couple of Chardonnays in a relentlessly Burgundian style — medium-bodied, crisp and oaky. Most of them possess elegance, too, and flavor to spare. At under seven dollars, they're all worth trying.

THE TOP 10
JOHANNISBERG RIESLINGS

It does seem sometimes that any discussion of a California wine type has to start with an explanation of nomenclature, and Johannisberg Riesling is no exception. It should really be called White Riesling, but it's probably too late now.

Back in the late 1800s a lot of people in the Napa Valley made wine called "Riesling" from the Sylvaner grape, which is not a member of the Riesling family at all. When the confusion got straightened out, much later, and plantings of White Riesling were increasing, something had to be found to differentiate the true Riesling, and since Schloss Johannisberg was the best-known German Riesling, the label was applied — and stuck.

For many years, California Johannisberg Rieslings didn't resemble German Rieslings at all; they were heavier, drier and higher in alcohol than the Rhines and Mosels, and were perhaps closer to Alsatian Rieslings. Too many, in my opinion, were also marred by a sharp aroma like acetone, and a slight citric bitterness under the fruit flavors.

With the advent of cold fermentation, it was possible to get more fruitiness into the wine; then, winemakers began lowering the alcohol content. Soon the California Johannisberg Rieslings were moving closer to their German cousins. Given differences in soil, climate, etc., they will never be the same, but they have become glorious delights in their own right these last few years, and will probably get even better.

The best are a complex blend of sweet fruitiness and the tang of acidity, with the freshness of a ripe melon and an almost floral aroma. They're fine for summer-afternoon sipping by themselves, or matched with chicken dishes prepared simply. The thoroughly sweet versions are covered in another section.

BERINGER WINERY. This Napa Valley winery's "Trauben-gold" is an astonishing bargain at under three dollars. It is legally entitled to be called Johannisberg Riesling; it also may include a little Muscat in the blend. Whatever, it is a medium-sweet and fruity wine with just the right smack of acid on the tongue. Non-vintage.

CHATEAU ST. JEAN. Richard Arrowood, the winemaker, insists on making most of his wines in small lots, labelled with the individual vineyard appellation; thus, we have the Robert Young Vineyard, Belle Terre Vineyard, and so on. It would be maddening to search out specific wines if he didn't make them all so good that in many cases it doesn't matter which one you get. Even his Sonoma/Mendocino blend is good. Prices range from around five to six dollars for these lively medium-sweet wines, and they are worth it.

HILLS CELLARS. A new Napa Valley winery, which will become Grgich-Hills soon, as the fabled winemaker from Chateau Montelena, Mike Grgich, has become a partner. He made some excellent Rieslings there, and Hills has some excellent ones already, so it seems a perfect marriage. Just over four dollars, with limited availability, this golden, tart wine is worth searching for.

CHARLES KRUG WINERY. One of the style-setters, this light and slightly sweet wine is a charmer. Both the 1975 and 1976 vintages are still around, at under five dollars; they share an excellent fruit-acid balance and melon-freshness.

LOUIS MARTINI WINERY. Widely known for his excellent and inexpensive reds, Martini also makes one of the better dry Johannisberg Rieslings. There is an intriguing spiciness to its flavor, and at under four dollars it's a bargain.

ROBERT MONDAVI WINERY. The 1975 vintage is terrific, and the 1976 is great; open a bottle, and within minutes the aroma fills the room. Medium-sweet, it manages to possess a flavor that is both lush and fresh at the same time. It is five dollars a bottle, and it is worth it.

THE MONTEREY VINEYARDS. The 1974 debut vintage for this winery was a winner, and the 1975 is another. It is slightly sweet and a little lighter than most of the others, but no less flavorful. Under four dollars.

JOSEPH PHELPS VINEYARDS. Another new Napa Valley winery, blessed with a German winemaker who knows how to get the best out of this grape. Past vintages have been excellent, and the 1975, currently available though in short supply, upholds the standard. An elegant, complex and sturdy wine, medium-sweet, with a tinge of pleasant earthiness. Around five dollars.

SAN MARTIN VINEYARDS. Another German winemaker, Ed Friedrich, is doing great things in Santa Clara and Monterey (the grape acreage is scattered). The winery is relatively small and the grapes come from different areas, leading to some unevenness from vintage to vintage, but they've all been good enough to merit attention. The 1976 now on the market is a trifle tart, which should smooth out with a little more time in the bottle; around four dollars. There is also a "Soft" Johannisberg Riesling in short supply that is low in alcohol (around 10%) and so high in flavor that a sip is a mouthful.

SONOMA VINEYARDS. One of the first wineries to attempt more of a German style and to lower the alcohol levels (to about 11.5% right now). The 1975 and 1976 are medium-sweet, golden and soft, and quite a bargain at under four dollars.

THE TOP 10 — LATE-HARVEST RIESLINGS

One of the least attractive sights in the world is a bunch of shriveled-up grapes covered with the thick gray mold called *botrytis cinerea,* but winemakers are always delighted at its appearance. These ugly-duckling grapes will be quite beautiful vinous swans, you see.

As with opera, the English common version of the name is the worst: Noble rot. The Germans call it "Edelfaule," the French "poriteurre noble." Most California producers refer to it on the labels as "Late Harvest," as the grapes are left longer on the vines than normal.

What happens is that this beneficial mold attacks the grapes, pierces the skins and lets the water evaporate from the pulp, which has the effect of concentrating the sugars; this occurs around harvest time, and some further ripening results in grapes of astonishing richness, with a very distinct character. In France, it yields the great Sauternes, such as Chateau d'Yquem; in Germany, with the Riesling grape, the Ausleses and Spatleses. In America, it's Late Harvest Rieslings.

The flavor association most thought of here is a honeyed unctuousness, not cloying; some hints of ripe peaches can sometimes be discerned. And there is the subtle note of the botrytis character itself, which is difficult to define, but lovely. A number of the best regular Johannisberg Rieslings have hints of botrytis, which enrich them without edging too much toward sweetness.

These of course are dessert wines, or for warm afternoon sipping with special friends (the necessary dearness of the price dictates no casual popping of their corks). They'd go well with a fresh pear and Gourmandise cheese dessert.

Botrytis comes and goes; its flourishing depends on special weather conditions. There was a lot of it around in the 1976 and 1977 harvest, so if you see any by the people noted here, snap them up — they've proved that they know how to handle the tricky mold.

ALMADEN VINEYARDS. Late Harvest. You don't have to be a small winery tucked back in the mountains to make a fine wine, as this one proves. The 1975 vintage was excellent, and at just under six dollars, a bargain. A wild-flower nose and honey-sweet flavor, a little light in body, and a six percent sugar level — quite sweet.

BERINGER WINERY. Late Harvest. Merely sweet (about four percent sugar), and the least expensive at under five dollars, the golden wine has a perfumey, almost apple-like nose and ripe-apricot sort of flavor. The winemaker, Myron Nightingale, has made some of California's most impressive late-harvest wines.

BURGESS CELLARS. Selected Late Harvest. The 1976 version is merely the latest of several winners from this winery. Full-bodied and elegant, with a nice acid undertone that insures it can stand a little more time in the bottle and reach its peak in a year or two as a mellow and rewarding wine — a Mr. Pickwick of a wine, if you will. Just under ten dollars.

CHATEAU ST. JEAN. Selected Late Harvest. As usual, a plethora of vineyard names here to confuse or delight you. All of the Selected Late Harvest wines are sweet (from four to over six percent sugar) and very well made, with reminiscences of honey and ripe apricots and flowers in the aromas, and velvety lushness in the flavors; they are also around eight dollars, and they are all worth it. The winery also makes two sweeter and richer versions, at twenty-five and forty dollars.

FIRESTONE VINEYARD. Late Harvest. The 1976 is a beauty, with a properly rich botrytis flavor underlying the full fruitiness. Nice, honeyed aroma and medium sweetness. Under eight dollars.

FREEMARK ABBEY. Sweet Select. This winery made perhaps the best late harvest Riesling in California, the legendary 1973 "Edelwein," which helped start the whole joyous trend. This version is straightforward and quite good. It has an earthy undertaste which is odd but not unattractive — it sometimes crops up in botrytised wines — and it has a good full mouth-feel and underlying acid. At just under seven dollars, not bad.

GEYSER PEAK. Late Harvest. This Sonoma winery started with an unimpressive line of jug wines, but has lately been moving into high gear with their newest varietals. This one is a beauty, in limited supply, but quite reasonably priced at under five dollars. It's medium sweet and subtle, even a trifle understated, but a very good sipper.

HACIENDA WINE CELLARS. The wine has a floral, honeyed aroma and full body; not overly sweet, but quite complex. The finish is a trifle short — an awkward but intriguing wine. Under six dollars.

JOSEPH PHELPS VINEYARDS. Selected Late Harvest. This wine is very sweet (around ten percent sugar), very expensive (around twenty-one dollars) and very, very good. The Riesling character comes through right along with a wild-honey scent, and perfect acid balance gives it liveliness. The flavor stays and stays. This is one wine you can smell across the room, and it will surely lead you by the nose. Hard to find, but worth the search and the price. 1975 vintage.

SAN MARTIN VINEYARDS. Special Edition. The 1976 vintage was a beauty, about eight percent sugar, low in alcohol, with an almost citrus tang somewhere in among the honeyed flavors. Withal, it has a friendly smoothness and softness, and, at under six dollars, it's a bargain.

THE TOP 10 ──────────
CHENIN BLANCS ──────

Chenin Blanc is much like Zinfandel, in that it is very popular and made in different styles. It is also a very agreeable wine, easy to like in whatever form it takes.

The "classic" style, which has been around for all of thirty years, has been to make the wine light, fruity and somewhat sweet — good warm-afternoon sipping wine. There are so many acres of Chenin Blanc vines planted that it has turned up as an enhancement in many jugs of California Chablis, too.

Lately some ambitious winemakers have been turning out a dry version, while endeavoring to preserve the fruitiness, giving us a nicely rounded wine to go with meals. There have even been versions aged in oak, which were decidedly odd, but interesting. The charms of Chenin Blanc are considerable, however, and the wine persists in being quite agreeable in both dry and slightly sweeter versions.

Being a light wine, Chenin Blanc goes best with food like chicken; as it's somewhat less acidic than other wines, it wouldn't be the best match with fish or shellfish or anything cloaked in a rich sauce.

There are probably a hundred Chenin Blancs in California, and they are rarely expensive, making it an easy category to explore.

BURGESS CELLARS. This is one of the dry ones, really very much of a dinner wine. Straw-colored, with a subtly perfumed aroma, it is quite full and crisp in the mouth. Over four dollars.

DRY CREEK VINEYARD. This one tends slightly to the austere side, with a slight but pleasant bitterness in the finish. The style has been changing, and recent versions are much more appealing. Good dry dinner wine, under four dollars.

KENWOOD VINEYARDS. One of the more consistently satisfying dry versions comes from this Sonoma winery, just hitting its stride. Pale and somewhat delicate, the wine nevertheless offers excellent flavor; it just sort of sneaks up on you. Just over three dollars.

CHARLES KRUG WINERY. This is the winery that started the whole Chenin Blanc idea, and it continues to be a soft and slightly sweet beauty, with enough flavor to be versatile — try it alone, or with a light lunch, such as chicken salad. Under four dollars.

MIRASSOU VINEYARDS. A little sweeter than most, this wine provides fine sipping; while the first impression of flavor is sweetness, you soon realize that it is the intense fruitiness that is leading you astray (and making you smile). A lovely wine, under four dollars.

ROBERT MONDAVI WINERY. When Bob Mondavi was at Charles Krug, Chenin Blanc was his idea, and he has taken it a little further at his own winery over the years. The wine is fresh and fruity and refreshing, and the slight sweetness is balanced nicely by a touch of bite from bottling under pressure — almost imperceptible bubbles dance on your tongue. Under four dollars from honest retailers; others, aware of its raging popularity, charge what the traffic will bear.

PARDUCCI WINE CELLARS. From Mendocino comes this rather sturdy and even tart dry wine offering a good idea of what the Chenin Blanc flavor ought to be. At just over three dollars, it's a bargain.

SAN MARTIN VINEYARDS. A blend of Santa Clara and Monterey grapes, this wine is full, almost opulent, in its charms, very slightly sweet. It's just over three dollars. The winery also produces a "soft" version, at ten percent alcohol, which is very lush and fruity, but a trifle over-priced at five dollars the bottle.

STAG'S LEAP VINEYARD. This small Napa winery produces just two wines, and this is an excellent version of one of them — dry and full, yet light and balanced and crisp. Four dollars.

STERLING VINEYARDS. In the past, a bit of Chardonnay was blended in, which gave the wine rather more backbone and toughness than expected in a Chenin Blanc. Subsequent versions have been a trifle softer, but still full-flavored and dry, though never quite a typical Chenin Blanc. Under five dollars.

THE TOP 10
SAUVIGNON BLANCS

Sauvignon Blanc was highly thought of by a few winemakers and other experts but ignored by consumers until, just over ten years ago, Robert Mondavi renamed it Fumé Blanc and proved that a wine by any other name could sell better.

In the intervening years, we have had all sorts of variations, like Blanc Fumé, Pouilly Fumé, Blanc de Sauvignon, etc. But now, with proper popularity, winemakers are generally feeling secure enough to let the wine fly under its own banner; most call it Sauvignon Blanc, and a few others call it by a Fumé designation.

The grape is a cousin of Cabernet Sauvignon, and has much the same herbacious, fresh-grass undertone to the flavor, very distinctive and very pleasant. Made dry with good acidity, it is a rival to the more expensive Chardonnay; it matches the same sort of foods, that is to say full-flavored seafood, chicken with complex sauces, game birds and even light meats like veal.

As more acreage comes into bearing, especially in Monterey County, more and more names will enter the lists. Even now Almaden has produced a Monterey Sauvignon Blanc that is excellent and inexpensive, though in short supply. And the Monterey Vineyard has brought out a botrytised version, not quite the same as Sauternes, but sweet and luscious and fine on its own terms.

In the hands of the brothers Gallo, it has also become a hallmark wine in larger supply than most wineries can hope to offer. Recent bottlings of their Sauvignon Blanc have been quite nice, and true to type, though somewhat subdued in character; still, at under two dollars, it's a good place to start.

There was a time, before it got to be a hot item, when vintages were around long enough to be discussed; now, the wines come and go awfully fast. Sometime this year, Sauvignon Blanc from last year appears and disappears, and one must wait for the next vintage. Thus, in 1978, we will see the 1977 vintages appearing; if you see a 1976, grab it and drink it soon, while you wait for any 1977s you were lucky enough to find to age; the wine does improve in the bottle for a while, softening and gaining some complexity.

51

CALLAWAY VINEYARDS. The cool climate of Temecula belies Southern California's image, and seems to suit Sauvignon Blanc just fine, if this wine is any index. The color is pale, but the body and flavor are full, even sturdy. Five dollars.

CHATEAU ST. JEAN. This is a very crisp and assured version of Sauvignon Blanc, with an almost puckery tartness underlying the full and complex flavors. The lightly perfumed aroma is a lovely bonus. Over six dollars.

CHRISTIAN BROTHERS. The name is Blanc Fumé, and it is a bargain at just over three dollars. The wine does possess a little less varietal character and complexity than some of the others, but it is dry and sturdy and flavorful nonetheless.

DRY CREEK VINEYARDS. This wine has been notable since the first vintage, in 1971. David Stare may have the vineyards, or the talent, or both. But whichever, he makes a notable Fumé Blanc. It's full-bodied and definitely grassy in flavor, and does improve in the bottle for a year or two after the vintage. Just over five dollars.

FOPPIANO VINEYARDS. Once a year, usually in late Spring, this Sonoma winery releases its Sonoma Fumé, and it disappears as quickly as a clever bigamist. It's tart, flavorful and nicely rounded, and a bargain at under five dollars.

ROBERT MONDAVI WINERY. The first is still the best. Mondavi's Fumé Blanc may be the most dependable, tasty white wine made in California. Somehow it combines sugar/acid balance and varietal character, and adds an extra dimension of suppleness to come up with a wine that is quite elegant and refreshing. Just over five dollars, and always a bargain.

SAN MARTIN VINEYARDS. This Sauvignon Blanc is in a different style than most, but no less attractive. It's light, with a touch of spritz on the tongue, and slightly less tart than the others. Withal, it's a pleasant sipper with enough character to accompany light foods, and a good buy at under four dollars.

SPRING MOUNTAIN VINEYARDS. This is another elegant, weedy/grassy, dry and tart delight; with a year or two of bottle age, it can rival most any other white as a match with the best fish or shellfish. Just over five dollars.

STERLING VINEYARDS. This rivals the Mondavi in complexity and elegance, being bone-dry and forcible, full of varietal character and tartness, yet fresh and amiable. It'll not only stand up to rich food, it'll talk back; five dollars.

WENTE BROTHERS. Flavors are a little subdued, and the winery always seems to release the wine a little late (like two years after the vintage, so you have to drink it right away, and in the past it was sometimes a little over the hill). The white-wine boom has led to earlier release of the wine, which greatly benefits its admirers. The wine is dry, fresh and verges on the austere, though the varietal character is ever so slightly subdued. It's a bargain at under three dollars.

"Gewurz" (gee-wurts) means "spicy" in German, and that's the principal element in the flavor of these agreeable white wines — a quite aggressive spiciness. The grape has been most notable in Alsace, where the wines are a perfect foil for the rich and spicy Alsatian foods, especially goose-liver patés and wonderful sausages; the Alsatian style tends toward relatively high alcohol (nearly thirteen percent) and a dryness that brings out the spice even more.

Some California winemakers have gone the Alsatian route, but more and more have lately tended to go for a softer and slightly sweeter style that is winning more and more fans. To get the wine made just right, it is said that the pickers have to just about sleep in the vineyards, to get the grapes at just the right, brief moment of ripeness and spiciness; in addition, the wine takes some care in the making. What all this translates out to for you is that the wine is never cheap; but it is frequently worth it.

It's such a striking wine that it doesn't go well with a lot of foods, but is a good accompaniment to light lunches, such as quiches or crab and shrimp dishes. It's also superb as an aperitif, along with paté and cheeses.

ALMADEN VINEYARDS. Special Selection. The Almaden Special Selections are always vintage-dated and sometimes hard to find; the 1974 currently available is a real bargain at just over three dollars. Medium-bodied, with a moderate spiciness, it's a good wine to begin your Gewurztraminer explorations with; the non-vintage version is somewhat blander but not bad, and under three dollars.

BUENA VISTA. A Sonoma-Mendocino blend, it's a little pricey at almost six dollars, but still a very nice wine in the 1975 version. A flowery-spicy aroma is followed by a tingle of spritz on the tongue; the clean, spicy flavor is lingering and lovely.

CHATEAU ST. JEAN. The 1975 version may be the best in its style so far. Though it's a big wine in some ways, it still possesses a silky elegance and very slight sweetness, with almost a citrus undertone in the flavor. Around six dollars, and worth it.

GRAND CRU VINEYARDS. This small Sonoma winery has been doing some extraordinary things, and their Gewurz-traminers have been some of them from the start. The 1975 is a winner, with a full and floral nose, medium body and a sweet/spicy finish on the tongue that is the nicest one-two punch you'll ever get. At under five dollars, a steal.

LOUIS MARTINI WINERY. This Napa winery has been at the Gewurztraminer game longer than anybody else, and in the dry style, nobody does it better; at under four dollars, it's also a bargain. It has all the spice it ought to, and the nice fruity flavors are balanced with a pleasantly bitter taste in the finish. This would go with more foods than the others.

MIRASSOU VINEYARDS. From Monterey County comes this winner, in the slightly sweet style. Around four dollars, it's a fine example of fruit/spice/acid balance and somewhat full body, altogether refreshing.

PEDRONCELLI WINERY. The 1975 version from this Sonoma County winery is a little subdued compared to its earlier incarnations, but still quite good and affordable at under three dollars. It has a lovely gold color, and the spice comes through well on the palate for a clean, lingering finish. A bit less sweet than some of the others, this is also a good wine with food.

JOSEPH PHELPS VINEYARDS. Perhaps the fact that this Napa winery has a German winemaker helps account for the above-average quality of its Gewurztraminers. This is a complex wine, with acid, fruit, spice and a touch of sweetness coming together like a great string quartet — and the music lingers on your palate.

SIMI WINERY. For some time, Simi Gewurztraminers have been one of the benchmarks; the 1975 version continues to uphold the standard. The aroma is almost musky, and the sugar/acid balance is perfect. It seems light at first, but the flavors keep coming back at you, and it can hold its own against sausages.

WENTE BROS. From Monterey County, this wine is odd but quite attractive. It has an almost citrus undertone in the taste that is pronounced, along with a pleasantly firm acidity. Sweetness is more in the background here and, although it's medium-bodied, it seems light because of the slightly peculiar style. Best as an aperitif. Under five dollars.

THE TOP
BLANCS DE NOIR

This is a relatively new category in California, quite popular, maybe even a fad, but still delightful. Blancs de Noir are white (or almost white) wines made from red grapes. In France they were also known as "oeil de perdrix" (eye of the partridge) for their delicate hue — paler than Rosé.

The most successful versions have been made from Pinot Noir grapes, although Sutter Home makes an attractive White Zinfandel. During the 1977 harvest, a cool spell resulted in Pinot Noir being harvested in some places at a lighter stage of development, which will undoubtedly result in quite a few more of these wines this year.

They are usually fairly dry, slightly tart and delicate; they are also delightful, as mentioned earlier. Three wines have been around long enough to have established some sort of track record, and shouldn't be overlooked.

CAYMUS VINEYARDS. The first consistent Pinot Noir Blanc in California, a lovely, fresh and fragrant wine.
Under five dollars.

SEBASTIANI VINEYARDS. This one made a big splash a few years ago and has gotten lighter and better since. Gus calls it Eye of the Swan, and he should know — he's also an ornithologist. Under four dollars, and a bargain.

CHATEAU ST. JEAN. This Blanc de Noir is well-made, perfumey, and delicately complex. At just under six dollars, a bit pricey.

THE TOP 10
MISCELLANEOUS WHITE WINES

A few wines are for the thinking, most are for the drinking. There are any number of wines with their own identities, in categories or amounts too small to be lumped with any other, which should not be overlooked. Here are ten such, good wines that demand nothing more than to be enjoyed. They have delighted in the past, current versions are good, and the future will undoubtedly be just as pleasant.

CHRISTIAN BROTHERS Chateau La Salle. This medium-bodied, golden wine is perfect for after dinner, a mate for fresh fruit and light cheese. Essence of Muscat is the idea, and it works perfectly — sweet and spicy. Under three dollars.

CONCANNON VINEYARDS Muscat Blanc. Like Gewurztraminer, Muscat varieties (it's a complicated family tree) have a certain spiciness, and usually a bit of sweetness. These are lazy summer afternoon sipping wines, and the Concannon version is the best of them, light and flowery and reasonably priced at under four dollars a bottle.

GALLO French Colombard. This grape was always a lowly one, destined for blends and showing up as a main component in California Chablis. On its own, it can make an agreeable, somewhat tart wine. The Gallo version is balanced with some sweetness, fresh and clean and a bargain at under two dollars.

LOUIS MARTINI WINERY Folle Blanche. This is the only version of this variety (meaning "crazy white" in French) in California; in France, the wine is distilled into Cognac. For those who prefer to sip drier wines, it's a pleasant change of pace.

PAUL MASSON Emerald Dry. This wine is made from the Emerald Riesling grape, which is a cross between two other varieties developed by the University of California at Davis. Some hints of its Muscat parentage come through in a subdued floral nose, while there is also an undertone of clean Riesling character coming through. Basically, it's clean, tart and pleasant, and sells for under three dollars.

SAN MARTIN VINEYARDS Emerald Riesling. This is a light, crisp version of a rare wine, worth looking for. Floral aroma and light body, with an intriguingly soft flavor—the clean and fruity aftertaste sneaks up on you. Around three dollars.

SONOMA VINEYARDS French Colombard. Somehow Rod Strong found a way to make this wine fairly dry without yielding to the hazard of bitterness this variety can spring on you when the sugar gets low. Perhaps it's the very faint touch of wood that steadies the balance; at any rate, it's tart and dry and reasonable at under three dollars.

SOUVERAIN OF ALEXANDER VALLEY Colombard Blanc. This moderately dry wine from upper Sonoma County may be the best around in its variety. Clean, fresh, medium-bodied, its tartness marries well with the slightest perceptible tinge of sweetness. Good with food or all alone. Under three dollars.

WENTE BROS Blanc de Blancs. A blend of Chenin Blanc and a variety called Ugni Blanc, this slightly sweet wine has been a favorite for years. Snobs sneer at it as a "beginner's wine," but I like to think of it as delightfully uncomplex.

WENTE BROS Dry Semillon. There are not many varietal Semillons available, and this estate-bottled, bone-dry wine is certainly the best. It tends to crisp acidity and rounded grapiness, and goes well with fish. Under four dollars.

THE TOP 10 —————
JUG WHITES —————

Like their red cousins, California jug white wines have been
moving toward dryness and more character, but a little more
slowly; it seems that when people talk about wanting dry wines
it is different from what they actually want to taste.

Nevertheless, there is good news from the jug field, and
that is that there is plenty of rewarding activity going on; quite
a few of the wines on this list are newcomers one way or the
other, which bodes well for the future.

There are no Rhine or Sauterne types listed here, as all
seem too light, indistinct in character and a tad too sweet and
low in acid — just plain flabby wines.

JAMES ARTHUR FIELD Chablis. There really is a
J. A. Field, and he buys wine in bulk, then blends it till it suits
his taste, and bottles it. Some batches are better than others,
but most have been very good, and a bargain at under three
dollars for a half-gallon.

GALLO Sauvignon Blanc. This is probably the driest white
wine Gallo makes, and the best. It has good, if subdued,
varietal character in its fresh and lively flavor. Just over three
dollars a magnum.

KENWOOD VINEYARDS Chablis. This wine has always had a lot of character and sturdiness. It's dry and medium-bodied, with pleasant fruitiness; goes well with food. Under three dollars a magnum.

CK MONDAVI Chablis. An old standby for many years, the wine offers fresh, clean flavors. Not much character, just a straightforward, refreshing sipper. Under four dollars the half-gallon.

ROBERT MONDAVI White Table Wine. This wine is a blend of several grapes, very well made, with engaging fruitiness and complexity. Dry and a trifle soft. Under three dollars for a magnum.

PARDUCCI WINE CELLARS Chablis. This wine is vintage-dated and slightly different from the non-vintage — and slightly higher-priced, at just over three dollars a magnum. It's still a very good buy, with a lively flavor and pleasant hint of tartness.

PEDRONCELLI WINERY Sonoma White. A golden, medium-bodied dry and fruity wine with good acid balance, it's a good buy at just over three dollars.

SONOMA VINEYARDS French Colombard. The 1977 vintage is out now, and it's a beauty — fresh and flavorful, nicely balanced with acid, quite well-made wine. Over four dollars a magnum.

SONOMA VINEYARDS Chenin Blanc. This one is also vintage-dated, and the 1977 is also a winner. It is slightly more sweet than the French Colombard, but the acid balance comes through for a fresh and lively flavor. Over four dollars a magnum.

STERLING VINEYARDS White Table Wine. A dry wine with a lot of character, maybe a touch of Chardonnay in the blend, a slight oakiness. An ambitious wine, and it delivers. Over four dollars a magnum.

THE TOP 10 ROSÉ WINES OF CALIFORNIA

THE TOP 10
ROSÉS

Pink wines don't have very good standing in the wine world, perhaps because they're thought of as the "compromise" wines, or the little wines for the little ladies. If we can pull aside the curtain of snobbery long enough, it will be discovered that there are some interesting wines here with excellent flavors that should not be overlooked.

The same sort of restless experimenting that has gone on with other wine types in California has gone on with Rosés. The wines I have chosen here are all varietal Rosés, for the simple reason that most of the generic Rosés, and even most of the Grenache Rosés, are cloyingly sweet and frequently too thin.

Rosés from good varieties possess most of the same qualities that make their darker cousins fine, but in a more subdued sort of way. The wines are fermented only a short time on the skins, which gives them color and tannins; they are then drawn off to continue fermentation as mere juice. They should be consumed young and chilled, and are a good accompaniment to light meats like chicken, pork and even ham.

Those I have cited are fairly dry. Vintage dates are important only as an index of age; they should be consumed young. They are all under four dollars.

DRY CREEK Rosé of Cabernet Sauvignon. Rather dry, with a hint of fresh-grass flavor inherited from the variety. The color is a light and lively pink.

FIRESTONE VINEYARD Rosé of Cabernet Sauvignon. A trifle sweeter than the Dry Creek, with a more pronounced roseate hue. Plenty of fruity flavor here.

MONTEREY VINEYARDS Rosé of Cabernet Sauvignon. Brilliant dark-pink color and a refreshing bite of acidity liven this wine.

SIMI WINERY Rosé of Cabernet Sauvignon. Fresh and appealing, round and gentle flavors — everything it ought to be.

ROBERT MONDAVI WINERY Gamay Rosé. More of a delicate salmon tint to the pink color of this wine, with the refreshing quality of the Gamay flavor shining through.

HEITZ CELLARS Grignolino Rosé. A definite orange tint to this tart, dry wine, with enough acid and flavor to cut through light tomato sauces or sausages.

MIRASSOU VINEYARDS Petite Rosé. Made from Petite Sirah grapes, this wine is less dry than some of the others, with plenty of fruit and rich flavor.

SIMI WINERY Rosé of Pinot Noir. One of the more successful and better varietal Roses, this one will spark plenty of imitators. Fresh and fruity, but with enough astringency to make it a match for many light meats.

CONCANNON VINEYARDS Zinfandel Rosé. The label proclaims that the wine is dry, and the label does not lie. The bramble-berry flavor of the parent grape comes through well, providing plenty of taste. Very nice aroma, too.

PEDRONCELLI WINERY Zinfandel Rosé. A slight shade less dry than the Concannon, but no less berry-like and fruity, with a round, appealing taste.

THE TOP 10 SPARKLING WINES OF CALIFORNIA

THE TOP 10
SPARKLING WINES

Frenchmen get terribly incensed over the fact that we call our
sparkling wines Champagne; they started complaining right
after a California Champagne won a gold medal in France
just after the turn of the century, and they realized they had
competition.

There are three kinds of California Champagne, and all are
required by law to announce which they are on the label.
"Bulk Process" is made in bulk, usually slightly sweet, and what
you are liable to get at very large parties and receptions.
The "transfer" or "Charmat" method involves fermenting the
wine in the bottle, then transferring it to a large vat for clarifi-
cation of its sediment, then returning it to the bottle, which
reduces the cost of producing it; such wines are labeled with
either of the above terms, or "Fermented in *the* bottle," which
can cause some confusion with the true "methode Champenois."

The best Champagne (the *true* Champagne, to a Frenchman) is kept in the same bottle throughout, and has to be
tended by hand through its several stages, which is why it costs
more, but also why it's so good. The label announces it:
"Fermented in *this* bottle."

Champagne is actually fermented twice, and it is the
second fermentation, in a closed container and preferably the
bottle, that yields the delightful bubbles. During the second
fermentation, the best wines are stored with the corks pointed
down. As the fermentation proceeds, dead yeast cells drop into
the neck of the bottle. The longer the wine stays "on the yeast,"
the more delicate flavors it acquires, and the better (smaller
and longer-lasting) the bubbles. When the fermentation is done,
the necks are frozen so that the yeast becomes a solid hunk
which is then removed. A little grape sugar, brandy and wine
will be added to top up the bottle and adjust its sugar and
alcohol content, and it is ready.

The amount of sugar added determines whether it will be
"Natural" (bone-dry), "Brut" (softly dry), and "Extra Dry"
(actually perceptibly sweet), or "Demi-Sec" (quite sweet).

Once people have gotten used to the taste of bone-dry Champagne, they find it awfully difficult to go back to the sweet, unbalanced types. The dry versions actually have a pleasant hint of yeast in the aroma, like fresh-baked bread.

There are other sparkling wines worthy of note in California. Mirassou makes a sparkling Gamay Beaujolais that in good years is very good, and can claim to be America's only true Sparkling Burgundy. Papagni has made a sparkling Muscat that has been very popular, though it's rather sweet.

One important thing to note: Champagne should never be served in those terrible hollow-stemmed saucer-glasses. The whole idea is to enjoy the bubbles, and these glasses, with their wide surface area, only help dissipate them; a jelly glass would be better.

Most Champagnes — from anywhere — are non-vintaged. When you see a vintage date, it's intended to signify that the wine is special. Sometimes it is. Schramsberg is the only California winery that regularly does, and deserves to.

Incidentally, one reason for the high price of Champagne, both Californian and imported, is that the Government, in its infinite wisdom, taxes the devil out of it. No one really knows why, except that back in the days right after Repeal, some dimwit probably decided that it was a luxury, a rich man's drink, and a high tax was a good way to soak the rich (and also make it too expensive for poor folks who might have something to celebrate?). Someone even wrote a poem about that:

> *Here's to Champagne —*
> *It'll end all your troubles;*
> *A dollar's worth of wine*
> *And two for the bubbles.*

ALMADEN VINEYARDS. This mammoth winery has been making concerted efforts to upgrade its wines, and this new "Natural" Champagne is one excellent result. Made from the distinguished Chardonnay grape, it is properly dry, acidic and very tasty, lacking only yeastiness. Around six dollars.

DOMAINE CHANDON Cuvee de Pinot Noir. Yes, Champagne is also made from red grapes, and this wine shows it in its lovely light bronze-pink color. Quite dry, full of subdued varietal flavor — very fruity. One of the best Champagnes in California, but as the parent company is French, they merely call it "Napa Valley Sparkling Wine." Under nine dollars, and worth creating a special occasion for.

DOMAINE CHANDON Brut. This wine is a blend of Pinot Noir, Pinot Blanc and Chardonnay. The color is pale gold, the aroma hints of yeast, and the flavor is delicate and complex. Under nine dollars.

KORBEL Brut. Perhaps the best-known and most widely distributed Champagne of California, and one of the most consistent. The winery also makes a good "Natural" version. Familiarity, in this case, should only breed affection; just over seven dollars.

HANNS KORNELL Sehr Trocken. This is a bone-dry, yeasty wine, very refreshing, with flavor and acidity in excellent balance. Just over seven dollars.

HANNS KORNELL Brut. A good example of the Brut style, similar to the Korbel but a little yeastier in the aroma and flavor. Just over seven dollars.

HANNS KORNELL Sparkling Muscat of Alexandria. This is, technically, not a Champagne, but its quality is so high it deserves to rank with these other wines. Slightly sweet, with the lovely floral aroma of Muscat, it is an excellent after-dinner wine, similar to the Italian Asti Spumante, but better than any in its price range. Around five dollars.

MIRASSOU VINEYARDS Au Natural. This is the other Champagne on the list made by a winery that doesn't specialize in that wine alone; Mirassou makes an extra effort with this one, and it pays off. Very dry and very yeasty. Under eight dollars.

SCHRAMSBERG Blanc de Blancs. In the Brut style, a blend of Pinot Noir and Chardonnay, this has been the preeminent California Champagne for a decade. It's very crisp, with a lovely straw color and good medium body. A full wine, but not heavy or ponderous. Under nine dollars.

SCHRAMSBERG Blanc de Noir. Also in the Brut style, made from Pinot Noir grapes, golden color and assertive flavor. This one can even improve with age. Under eleven dollars. Still the best California Champagne — if you can find it.

ODD BINS

THE TOP 10
WINERY TOURS

It is not true that if you've seen one winery — or had one winery tour — you've seen them all. But the principles of winemaking are pretty standard in many ways and, since most tours are concerned with the basics, they can get to be somewhat repetitious after a short while.

The best way to tour the wine country is to go to a winery that has a good tour and start the day with the whole works — a tour and tasting. From then on, just visit the tasting rooms. (Common sense should prevail, and you shouldn't schedule too many, whether or not you're driving.) Sometimes if a group is touring, you might have the tasting room almost all to yourself, and the winery employees will have more time to talk and explain things, especially if you display curiosity or knowledge. At any rate, one tour to start the day is a good brush-up on the principles of winemaking.

The wineries listed here generally have the most informative tour guides, are attractive, and pour good wines. There are a lot of wineries that attain two out of three of these criteria, and you may enjoy them too, but these have it all.

NAPA VALLEY

DOMAINE CHANDON. A jewel in Napa's crown, this Champagne (oops, sparkling wine — they're French and protective of the name) house is architecturally beautiful, contains a three-star restaurant run by a disciple of Paul Bocuse, and is staffed by young and intelligent tour guides. It's popular and the parking lot fills up frequently, so it's best during the week and first thing in the morning, which is easy, as it's at the bottom (south) end of the valley. No free tasting, but you can buy a generous glass of one of the marvelous Champagnes (oh, nuts to it) and enjoy it sitting in their attractive reception hall. On California Drive in Yountville, just off Highway 29.

ROBERT MONDAVI WINERY. Another architectural gem, this winery has only been open since 1966, but reflects the California Missions in its style. Inside, everything is modern, even ultra-modern, though in the end the wine ends up in the same sort of small oak barrels they use in France. The tour here is detailed and thorough, practically a short course in winemaking. Very popular — in summer, the tour buses pile up in the parking lot. On Highway 29, in Oakville.

STERLING VINEYARDS. All the way to the north end of the valley, and a beauty it is, modeled after a Greek monastery, perched atop a 600-foot-high knoll rising from the valley floor. Sterling is unique in that it has a self-guided tour — arrows point the way and story-board graphics tell you all about how wines are made; you travel up an aerial cable-car to the winery and are then on your own till you reach the tasting room. There is a charge of $2.50 for the ride, but you get it back if you buy a bottle of wine. The views of the valley are quite spectacular. 1111 Dunaweal Lane, Calistoga.

SONOMA

SEBASTIANI. This winery is not only popular, it's a historical landmark. The first part of the tour goes through the old part of the winery, and it's astonishing to suddenly enter a large room full of stainless steel tanks — like going from one century to another. Surrounded by vineyards and quite attractive and informal, much like the family. Another frequent sight is August Sebastiani himself, in bib overalls. 389 Fourth St., a few blocks past the town square in Sonoma.

SIMI WINERY. This is an old and charming winery, or perhaps one should say old-fashioned and charming. There isn't a lot to see, but the tour guides are especially good about explaining winemaking. The tasting room is one of the most attractive anywhere. 16275 Healdsburg Ave., Healdsburg, a short shunt from Highway 101.

SOUVERAIN OF ALEXANDER VALLEY. This striking winery is based on the design for hop kilns, which used to be one of the major agricultural endeavors in Sonoma before we lost our taste for really good beer. A good blend of modern and traditional inside; the tasting gallery has a lovely view of vineyards outside. There is also a restaurant which is pretty good. 400 Souverain Rd., Geyserville, just off 101.

MENDOCINO

PARDUCCI WINERY. Another blend of modern and traditional, with some of the nicest people you'll ever meet running the tours and tastings. The tasting room is extremely attractive, features stained-glass windows and a stone fireplace, and the grounds are beautifully landscaped. 501 Parducci Rd., Ukiah, just off 101.

SAN JOSE

ALMADEN VINEYARDS. The Santa Clara Valley has pretty much been swamped by creeping urbanization and the electronics industry, but Almaden holds out. It's one of America's biggest wineries, but the nicely landscaped grounds have a measure of serenity, and the tours are quite informative. There are also some good wines offered, to confound those who confuse size with quality. 1530 Blossom Hill Rd., San Jose.

SANTA BARBARA

THE FIRESTONE VINEYARD. Here is another reason to visit Santa Barbara; about 12 miles north of town is Los Olivos, and there is this new winery in the low, rolling hills of the Santa Ynez Valley. Modern, attractive and squeaky-clean. Zaca Station Rd., Los Olivos.

MONTEREY

THE MONTEREY VINEYARD. The basic style here is sort of modernized Mission, and the huge stained-glass windows help with the impression that you are in a shrine of wine. The guiding intelligence of Richard Peterson is evident everywhere, including the thoroughness of the tour guides' dialogue. Definitely worth the trip. 800 South Alta St., Gonzales.

THE TOP 10
TASTING ROOMS

What makes a good winery tasting room? To me it's a combination of attractiveness, comfort and no stinting on the wines — by which I don't mean a heavy hand with the pouring, but a willingness to pour a variety of wines, not just the ones a winery wants to push that month. And the person behind the bar should be informative and gracious.

Actually, most wineries possess all these features, and you really can't go too far wrong, as long as you remember that things do get hectic and crowded on summer weekends at some of the "showcase" wineries like Mondavi, Sterling, Christian Brothers and Sebastiani. If you must tour on summer weekends, that might be a good time to explore some of the lesser-known wineries — you can usually find some good bargains.

The following wineries were chosen because they rise above and beyond the call of duty.

NAPA

LOUIS MARTINI WINERY. The tasting room is large and subtly lighted, with a homey feel to it; chilled wines are taken out of a battered old refrigerator to be served. Although Martini's wines are widely available, the winery is one place to get some of his superb "Special Selection" and "Private Reserve" wines and some older wines, especially Pinot Noirs and Cabernets. Ask about the Moscato Amabile, an extraordinary light sweet wine that deserves its legend. It's right on Highway 29, at 245 St. Helena Hwy.

STERLING VINEYARDS. For the sheer experience of riding the aerial cable-car and the sweeping views of the valley from the beautiful tasting room, Sterling has to be included. As far as tastings go, they only pour about four of their wines and not always their fabulous ones; however, all their wines are pretty good, so you won't be shortchanged. If you're serious about buying wine, they will be more accommodating. 1111 Dunaweal Lane, Calistoga.

SONOMA

CHATEAU ST. JEAN. It really is a chateau, a beautiful Mediterranean-style villa among young vineyards (the winery proper is in another building). The walls are hung with the work of local artists, and the whole effect is really quite grand. The wines, mostly whites, follow through just as impressively as you might expect. 8555 Sonoma Hwy., Kenwood.

KENWOOD VINEYARDS. This winery is about as unimpressive and informal as you can get, but a lot of the wines are quite good, many of them real bargains. The tasting room has been prettified by a few hanging plants and a stained-glass window, but it still looks like the corner of a working winery, and it is. 9592 Sonoma Hwy., Kenwood.

PEDRONCELLI WINERY. This tasting room will never win any esthetic awards, but the people who pour are friendly, and the wines are superb and inexpensive, real winners. 1220 Canyon Rd., Geyserville.

SIMI WINERY. Stained glass and a lot of redwood make this a handsome room; the young ladies behind the tasting bar complete the picture. They also happen to be knowledgeable and charming. Simi has a lot of interesting wines, and this could be the place you make some gratifying discoveries. 16275 Healdsburg Ave., Healdsburg, a short jog off Hwy. 101.

SONOMA VINEYARDS. This winery is an architectural marvel built like a wheel, with the tasting room as its hub. You can walk around the circle and see the various phases of winemaking below in just a few minutes. Sonoma Vineyards had quite a number of wines and brands that have been discontinued, so that there are a lot of bargains here; actually, the regular line of their wines is quite varied and nicely priced too. 11455 Old Redwood Hwy., Windsor.

MENDOCINO

PARDUCCI WINE CELLARS. A quite attractive tasting room and nicely landscaped grounds make this a pleasant place to visit, but the wines overshadow all. Reasonably priced and well-made, they include a vintage-dated Chablis, French Colombard and a fresh and tasty Chardonnay. This is a good place to stock up. 501 Parducci Rd., Ukiah.

SANTA CLARA

MIRASSOU VINEYARDS. The walls are cool gray granite, but the people and the wines make it delightful anyway. The Mirassous are up to a lot of intriguing things with their wines, and this is a good place to check them out. The pace is unhurried and the mood is informal, especially if any of the large and apparently fun-loving Mirassou family pops in. 3000 Aborn Rd., San Jose.

SAN MARTIN VINEYARDS. This winery is exploding with new and excellent wines, made in small batches and hard to find, so you may as well go to the source. The tasting room is large and attractive, and tastings are conducted, rather than haphazard pouring, but there's nothing stuffy about it. 13000 Depot St., San Martin. Other tasting rooms around the state are in Morgan Hill, Gilroy, Camarillo, Monterey and Solvang, but the one at the winery is the best.

THE TOP 10 ─────
WINE-COUNTRY RESTAURANTS ──

The wine country of California is, sad to say, not a gastronomic paradise; most good chefs, it seems, would rather be down in San Francisco making twice as much money. Still, there are a lot of dedicated people trying very hard to make a go of country life and hospitality, so the future may be brighter than the present.

I have here concentrated on Napa, Sonoma and Mendocino; there are grapes grown elsewhere, and those regions deserve to be thought of as "wine country" too, but I have more complaints than compliments about their restaurants, for a variety of reasons. The places I cite have good food, good and reasonably priced wine lists, friendly service and a pleasant atmosphere.

NAPA

DOMAINE CHANDON. Simply the best restaurant in the valley, and reservations are imperative, even weeks in advance for dinner. French cuisine in the manner of Paul Bocuse. Not inexpensive, but worth every penny. On California Drive, Yountville.

LA BELLE HELENE. A small French restaurant in a stone building next to the Robert Louis Stevenson Museum. Very attractive, almost like dining in a castle; the menu is eclectic, reflecting the chef's mood, but always interesting. Lunch and dinner. 1345 Railroad Ave., St. Helena.

NAPA VALLEY CHEESE CO./MAMA NINA'S. By day, this little spot on Highway 29 just north of Yountville is a deli serving light lunches, and a good place for picnic supplies. At night, it becomes the Napa Valley extension of Mama Nina's, with simply superb homemade Italian food. Small and homey; an adventure. 7399 Highway 29, Oakville.

SILVERADO TAVERN. This is a family operation with a great dedication to wine; there is a wine-tasting bar, there are over a hundred wines on the wine list available at retail prices plus one dollar corkage, and they have regular wine-tastings on Friday nights. Otherwise, the emphasis is on steak, nicely done, and Wednesday is Zinfandel Beef night. 1374 Lincoln Ave., Calistoga.

SONOMA

AU RELAIS. A beautiful restaurant in a Victorian house on the edge of the town of Sonoma. Basically French, and don't overlook the crepes. Pleasant atmosphere and decor — the name means "rest stop," and they live up to it. 691 Broadway, Sonoma.

DEPOT HOTEL. A delightful openness is the hallmark of this architectural gem, actually a restored landmark. The food is excellent, too, but reservations are a must — the word is out. 241 First St. West, Sonoma.

HOFFMAN HOUSE. A small and charming country inn featuring good cooking and lots of it; almost like having dinner with a happy family. 21712 Old Redwood Highway, Geyserville.

MAMA NINA'S. This is my favorite Italian restaurant north of San Francisco, and it gives even the big-city places a run for the money. The pasta is homemade every morning, and the basil for the pesto sauce grows on the kitchen doorstep. Everything is good here, and you get a lot of it. Highway 101, one mile north of Cloverdale. Dinner only.

MENDOCINO

LEDFORD HOUSE. Seasonal menus, with some emphasis on seafood, prevail at this relaxed old restaurant. The fireplace and ocean view enhance the excellent food, imaginatively prepared. Highway 1, Little River, four miles south of Mendocino.

CAFE BEAUJOLAIS. Pastel wallpaper, oak tables and lots of fresh flowers begin the delight here, and the food completes it. The accent is French, and everything's fresh. Breakfast, lunch and dinner, reasonable prices. 961 E. Ukiah St., Mendocino.

NOTE: One other possibility, which doesn't fit any category, is the V. SATTUI WINERY, on Highway 29 in St. Helena. The tiny winery includes an excellent deli, where you can get meats, cheeses, fruit, bread, and of course wine, and repair to the picnic tables right outside, bordering vineyards. It is very, very nice on a sunny day.

THE TOP 10
PLACES TO STAY
IN THE WINE COUNTRY

Change is as constant in wine-country lodgings as it is with wines, it seems. Places I liked a lot a few years ago are gone, while new ones spring up like mushrooms after rain. Fortunately, there are enough good ones hanging in there, offering a variety of vacation styles.

NAPA

BURGUNDY HOUSE. This stone-walled inn stands amid vineyards at the southern end of the Napa Valley. The rooms are furnished with antiques; no private baths add to the rusticity. 6711 Washington St., Yountville.

MAGNOLIA HOTEL. Also furnished with antiques, though each of its six rooms does have a bath. Cozy and charming. The dinner is frequently good, too. 6529 Yount St., Yountville.

MOUNTAIN HOME RANCH. This is a mellow sort of resort, with tennis, swimming pool and hiking trails through the foothills of Mount St. Helena. Rustic summer cabins or modern cottages are available, and Granpa's Fried Chicken is the specialty on weekends. Mountain Home Ranch Rd., Calistoga.

NANCE'S HOT SPRINGS. People also come to Calistoga to take the waters, as they say; several hotels and motels offer mud baths, mineral tubs, sulphur steam baths and the like, and Nance's is the least like a medical facility. Homespun and old, but well-maintained. 1614 Lincoln Ave., Calistoga.

SILVERADO COUNTRY CLUB. At the other end of the scale (as well as the other end of the valley), you can have country-club living (and country-club prices). Cottages and apartments, quite nicely furnished, are spread through well-kept grounds. There is golf and tennis, air-conditioning and color TV, swimming pools and kitchens; there is also a restaurant. 1600 Atlas Peak Rd., Napa.

WINE COUNTRY INN. You can't get much closer to the
vineyards than at this inn, a beauty that combines stone and
wood in a handsome design. This has all the comforts, including
fireplaces in every room and great views. Antique furnishings,
of course. Expensive; great place for a second honeymoon.
1152 Lodi Lane, St. Helena.

SONOMA

HEXAGON HOUSE. The dining room really is six-sided, a
marvel of redwood and glass. The place is set back in the
forest, in a delightful setting. It has motel-style rooms but the
eighteen cottages away from the main building are best.
16881 Armstrong Woods Rd., Guerneville.

LONDON LODGE. The twenty-two-room motel is nothing
out of the ordinary, but the setting is — smack in the heart of
the Valley of the Moon, just below the entrance to Jack London
State Park (worth a visit). The setting is delightfully sylvan,
and the restaurant has a good bar and pretty good food.
13740 Arnold Drive, Glen Ellen.

LOS ROBLES LODGE. If all this rusticity isn't for you, you
might want to make your headquarters in the town of Santa
Rosa and confine your wine-touring to day trips. If so, this
well-run motel is just what you need. It's handy to Highway 101
and other wine-country roads, so you can get just about anywhere in Sonoma easily. The coffee shop is average, the dining
room pretty good. 925 Edwards Ave., Santa Rosa.

MENDOCINO

HERITAGE HOUSE. In one of the most beautiful settings in
the world — the Mendocino coast — nestles the compound of
cottages that make up Heritage House. Still more antiques,
of course; the cottages are charming and the grounds and
views are beautiful. A little expensive, and a little stuffy
(jackets and ties preferred at dinner). Little River, four miles
south of Mendocino.

NOTE: Mendocino has always had a number of good places to
eat, drink and stay. It has also always lacked stability and con-
tinuity in those areas; it is also, however, well worth a gamble.

THE TOP 10
WINE BOOKS

There are an awful lot of wine books on the market, ranging from the highly specific to the loosely general, and from the ridiculous (the majority) to the sublime.

The trouble with most wine books (including this one) is that no one knows it all. However, any combination of a couple of these will dovetail into all you need to know to be well-informed — plus a corkscrew, of course, as the real education and enjoyment is in bottles, not between covers.

There is one notable omission from this list: Frank Schoonmaker's "Encyclopedia of Wine." The late Mr. Schoonmaker compiled a beauty years ago, and it has gone through several editions; unfortunately, the last real revision took place more than ten years ago, and in many ways the book is obsolete. A new revision is promised this year, and it may well be worth looking into.

THE CALIFORNIA WINE BOOK, by Bob Thompson and Hugh Johnson. (Hardbound; William Morrow, New York, $15.95). I think the heavyweight Johnson is window-dressing for the less-well-known Thompson; the book is written in a graceful and easy-flowing style, and if there is anything Thompson has left out, I can't imagine what it might be. Half the book details the wineries, the other half the wines. Thompson is an optimist — his glass is always half-full rather than half-empty, but he provides a better feel for the people, wines and down-to-earth fun of it all than anybody.

THE WINES OF AMERICA by Leon Adams. (Hardbound; Houghton Mifflin, Boston, $10.95). Be sure you get the second edition, published this year. Adams must have visited every winery in the United States at least twice for this witty and comprehensive book. He's great on the history of wine in America (he's been involved in the wine trade for over 40 years), but he's right up to date on the latest wrinkle of winemaking in Texas, Michigan or wherever. If anyone qualifies for the title of the Boswell of American wine, it's him. Like Thompson, easy and good reading.

THE FIRESIDE BOOK OF WINE, edited by Alexis Bespaloff. (Hardbound, Simon & Schuster, New York, $12.95). This is an anthology of writing about wine — stories, songs, poems, essays, what have you, and it is delightful. You don't have to be an expert to appreciate the bawdy whimsy of Flanders and Swann's "Have Some Madeira, M'Dear," or Art Buchwald's account of his misadventures with wine. This is the kind of book that is best enjoyed like vintage Port, a little at a time.

CALIFORNIA WINE COUNTRY, by Bob Thompson.
(Paperbound; Sunset Books, Menlo Park, $3.95). The earliest
and still the best one-volume book on touring the wine
country, with a lot of other information on wine in general
tossed in. Excellent maps and good insights on where to go,
what to see and drink.

NAPA VALLEY WINE TOUR. (Paperbound; Vintage
Image, St. Helena, $5.95). This is a pretty complete book on
the wineries, inns and hotels, restaurants and winemakers
of Napa Valley, enriched by the pen-and-ink drawings
of Sebastian Titus. The text is just workmanlike, but it is a
comprehensive and attractive book.

SONOMA/MENDOCINO WINE TOUR. (Paperbound;
Vintage Image, St. Helena, $5.95.) A companion volume, this
one is just as thorough and attractive as the first one, though
the text is just as workmanlike. Titus's drawings are even a
little better this time — maybe the more varied Sonoma land-
scapes inspired him. In some ways Sonoma has more going for
it than Napa, unless you're a rabid grape nut, and this book
is just that much more interesting.

CENTRAL COAST WINE TOUR. (Paperbound; Vintage
Image, St. Helena, $5.95.) This volume covers wineries from
just south of San Francisco down to Santa Barbara, quite
a mixed bag of people and wines. At least this time the book is
quite well written, by Richard Hinkle, with good information
on restaurants and lodgings by William Gibbs. Almaden's
in here, and so is Ridge and the smallest commercial winery in
California. This charming guide to "the other wine country"
should make you feel adventurous.

*WINE: AN INTRODUCTION, by Maynard Amerine and
Vernon Singleton.* (Paperbound, University of California
Press, Berkeley and Davis, $5.95.) The authors were professors
at the UCD's famous school of enology for many years, and
are world-class experts. In a somewhat dry and precise way,
this book tells you all about what wine it, how it's made, and
what it ought to be like. Technical and sometimes tough going,
but worth it if you're serious about digging deeper.

THE COMMONSENSE BOOK OF WINE, by Leon Adams. (Paperbound; Dutton, New York, $3.95). Adams on wine in general takes on a tone a little like an evangelical preacher, but he's still fun to read. He tells you how to appreciate and use wine in a variety of situations and is either reassuring or mad as the devil, depending on whether he's telling you to drink wine out of a jelly glass if you feel like it, or whether he's complaining about restaurant markups on wine. "Commonsense" in this case is dead accurate.

GROSSMAN'S GUIDE TO WINES, SPIRITS AND BEERS, *edited by Harriet Lembeck.* (Hardbound; Scribner's, New York, $17.95.) Although there is a lot about spirits and a little about beer, and some things about restaurant and hotel operation — which is what this is a handbook for — this is one of the best one-volume books about what you drink there is, and the wine section is good and right up to date. Lembeck did her homework, and it shows, especially the California parts.

THE TOP WINE NEWSLETTERS AND MAGAZINES

We have to depart from the "Top 10" format a little bit here. Although there are dozens of wine newsletters and magazines, there simply aren't ten good ones.

The problem is that a newsletter can be a pretty inexpensive ego trip, and there are just as many ready-and-willing egos in the wine world as in an opera company. Outside of the collected speeches of almost any politician I can think of, you have never seen such balderdash, frequently illiterate, as these people will charge you to read. Not a chuckle or even a smile in the bunch, either — that sort of snob doesn't seem to know that wine is for the enjoying.

The following are by people who are honest and try hard to be accurate, thorough and non-boring, and generally succeed.

ROBERT LAWRENCE BALZER'S PRIVATE GUIDE TO WINE. This is the grand-daddy of wine newsletters, by the fellow who is probably the grand-daddy of wine columnists. Published monthly, but frequently late, like most of the others, it includes articles, ratings of featured wine types, gossip, news and good food recipes. Actors and other ardent amateurs join Balzer's panel of rating experts, which occasionally leads to offbeat recommendations, and his prose can be as purple as Petite Sirah, but the man knows his wines and loves them, and passes along both the knowledge and emotion quite gracefully; $18 for 11 issues annually — 12791 Newport Ave., Tustin, CA 92680.

CONNOISSEUR'S GUIDE TO CALIFORNIA WINE. This is probably the most thorough, if not exhaustive, newsletter on the subject. If there are 97 Zinfandels made in California, there's a good chance they'll all be reviewed here. One type is totally surveyed, tasted, analyzed and rated in each bimonthly issue, and there are articles about other aspects of wine wrapped around them. The judgments are fair, and the writing is easy, sometimes even entertaining; $15 for 6 issues annually — P.O. Box 11120, San Francisco, CA 94101.

FINIGAN'S PRIVATE GUIDE TO WINE. Robert Finigan is an arrogant and acerbic critic of wine; he's also rather good. Occasionally a trifle pompous, but he does have high standards and discovers good values. The newsletter is published monthly and is about the only one that comes out on time, but frequently devotes whole issues to expensive foreign wines, so if you're not a collector/connoisseur, he may not be for you; $20 for 12 issues annually — Walnuts & Wine, 100 Bush St., San Francisco, CA 94104.

VINTAGE. There are a few slick magazines devoted to wine, and this is the best of them, partly by default (the others are awful). Inconsistent in quality of its coverage, frequently late, laced with pompous editorial pronouncements by its publisher, the magazine still manages to be quite good most of the time due to a good stable of writers and in-depth special reports from its California editor; $20 for 12 issues annually — P.O. Box 2739, Boulder, CO 80302.

THE WINE SPECTATOR. This is a twice-a-month newspaper, mailed first class and always on time, about wine around the world. Mostly news about everything under the sun to do with wine that the editors can pack into its 16 pages — recipes with wine, tastings around the state, hard news, vintage reports, features, opinions, arguments — you name it, and they'll get it in, somehow, somewhere. It's lively and quite useful, the only publication of its kind in the United States, or maybe anywhere; $20 for 26 issues annually — 1930 Hornblend Ave., San Diego, CA 92109.

THE GRAPEVINE. Out of San Diego comes this engaging potpourri of tasting notes, evaluations and background articles on food and wine. It's an odd combination of seriousness and informality, like a banker in shirtsleeves. Eight times a year for $10; P.O. Box 22152, San Diego, CA 92122.

THE TOP
WINERY NEWSLETTERS

There are an awful lot of winery newsletters, but unless you're a stockholder or member of the winemaker's family, they're just not very interesting. Most are self-serving, frankly promotional tools, with a very narrow range of information, limited to current wines and glorification of the resident winemaker.

But there are some people who want to reach and teach people, and have the ability to write or the brains to hire someone who can. First, there is the Sebastiani family, and they are first by a long, long lead. Their newsletter is consistently informative, frequently entertaining and well-illustrated. And Mama Sylvia's recipes are sensational! They plug their wines, but not much at all — very soft sell.

All these are free.

SEBASTIANI VINEYARDS. Box AA, Sonoma, CA 94576.

CHARLES KRUG WINERY. A quarterly publication called "Bottles and Bins," this may be the oldest winery newsletter around. It's chatty — like a letter from an old friend in the Napa Valley, ruminating about this and that to do with wine. Good recipes included. Write P.O. Box 191, St. Helena, CA 94574.

SAN MARTIN VINEYARDS. The newsletter is called "The Organoleptic Evaluator," fancy talk for winetaster, but don't let that throw you. Ed Friedrich's intelligence and technical skill as a winemaker come through in a variety of ways that keep you interested. Write to 13000 Depot St., San Martin, CA 95046.

THE MONTEREY VINEYARD. Richard Peterson is a scientist as well as a good winemaker, so the thrust of his newsletter is technical, but the man also has a way with words and leavens everything with wit, and he doesn't ramble around. Write to 800 South Alta St., Gonzales, CA 93926.

SIMI WINERY. There's an equal blend of promotion and information in this newsletter, but the informational parts are done so well you can forgive the hard-sell. Write to 16275 Healdsburg Avenue, Healdsburg, CA 95448.

MIRASSOU VINEYARDS. Also an equal blend of promotion and information here, but they seem to be trying hard to communicate more and better; includes recipes. Write to P.O. Box 344, 3000 Aborn Road, San Jose, CA 95121.

THE TOP 10
WINE DRINKS

The first more-or-less modern wine drink was invented, if that's the right word, by the Germans. After a party, the servants would gather up all the flagons and carafes of wine and mead and whatever else was left over, and dump the remains into a large crock, which was then kept in the cold cellar and consumed later. It was called "Kalte Ende," cold ends. Some wit eventually dubbed it "Kalte Ente," which translates to "Cold Duck," and for reasons which escape me the name stuck. Today's version is a blend of sparkling wine and Concord grape juice, and it's probably no better than the old cold ends.

On the bright side, a good many ingenious people have worked long and hard to come up with a wonderful variety of delicious wine drinks — cold ones like flips and cobblers, many hot mulls and a variety of racy Champagne cocktails. Here are the best.

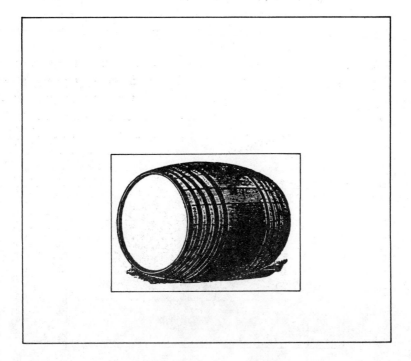

MIMOSA

The idea of combining Champagne and orange juice is so logical that one wonders why it's only been in the last 20 years or so that this drink has become popular. Maybe the fact that it's had a dozen or so names helped obscure its existence. Legend has it that it was first concocted in Florida, and that it was there named the Mimosa; as all the others names sound rather silly, I'm happy to go with it.

A few hints: The Champagne should be decent, and dry — Brut at least. It is obviously a waste of fine Champagne to use something like Domaine Chandon or Schramsberg, but don't sell yourself short with a sparkler you got for $1.98 either. Obviously, fresh orange juice is the best, but most other types will do almost as well.

Simply fill a wine glass two-thirds full, and top up with orange juice. One fifth-size bottle should serve four people nicely.

SPRITZER

The simple ideas are often the best, as the fellow who invented the paper-clip must have remarked at least once. A spritzer is a refreshing, light and low-calorie treat which is simply a combination of white wine and sparkling water, with a twist of lemon peel, over ice.

Since all the ingredients should be chilled already, you only need a couple of ice cubes in a tall glass. Pour it two-thirds full of white wine, add sparkling water and the twist, and enjoy. If you want to go first class (and why not?), use Perrier water instead of club soda. The Perrier bubbles are smaller and last longer, and don't bloat you up. It also seems to taste better.

A variation on this drink is the Rosé Spritzer, which is fine as long as the Rosé is reasonably dry. Otherwise, you might as well go for soda pop.

By the way, as the word comes from the German, it should be pronounced "shpritzer."

BLACK VELVET

The first half of the name is inaccurate — it's
dark brown — but the second half is perfect, for
this combination of Stout and Champagne
is smooth.

Stout is made from roasted hops, and is
heavier in body than ale or beer; it's got a
marvelously bittersweet, rich flavor that combines beautifully with the tart effervescence
of Champagne. As its flavor is so rich, almost
concentrated, it's good to remember that a little
goes a long way here. You can usually get
Stout in half-pint bottles, which is good unless
you're having a party; remember, however,
that Stout also contains alcohol.

Fill a wine glass nearly to the top (or six
ounces, depending on the size) with Champagne
and pour in a healthy ounce of Stout; you
don't need to stir, as the heavier Stout will mix
itself in. The color should be a deep brown, and
you should be able to see light through it.

SANGRIA

Sangria is best made with dry red wine, not something faintly sweet with some citrus juices premixed in, but not your best Cabernet Sauvignon either. A good, sturdy, inexpensive Zinfandel or Gamay Beaujolais would work fine or, for a large group, any dry red jug wine.

The subject of adding spirits to Sangria is confused and even controversial; I've seen recipes calling for a dollop of everything from Calvados to Galliano, and was once served "Sangria" in the Caribbean which was laced liberally with rum and garnished with apple slices. It was revolting.

A spirit is added for the flavor, not to fortify the drink; the only spirit that harmonizes with wine is its offspring, brandy, and very little goes into good Sangria. It should tiptoe across your tongue, not stomp.

    1 bottle (fifth) dry red wine
    2 limes or 1 lemon
    1 ounce brandy
    1 (10-oz.) bottle club soda
    1 orange
    sugar to taste

Pour wine into pitcher, squeeze in juice of limes or lemon, and half the orange, reserving the other half as slices for a garnish; add brandy. Taste and add a little sugar if desired, up to two teaspoons. Just before serving, add club soda and orange slices. Serve in tall glasses with just a few ice cubes.

CHAMPAGNE COCKTAIL

This drink was probably invented by the British. Besides being inveterate dabblers in drinks, they also seemed to have a mystical faith in Bitters — they mixed it with Gin, which did improve the flavor of the stuff, but they also mixed it with Dry Sherry, which is barbarous.

Whoever was responsible came up a winner with the Champagne Cocktail, however; the flavor is at once subtle but definite.

You need sugar cubes for this one. A teaspoon of sugar won't work, as the flavor depends on the slow-release effect of the dissolving cube.

Place a cube of sugar in the bottom of a Champagne glass; splash on Angostura Bitters till the cube is saturated, then fill the glass with Champagne. Don't stir, the bubbles will do your work for you, slowly.

KIR

This drink is named for Canon Kir, a distinguished Frenchman. It's a mixture of white wine and black-currant liqueur (cassis), although it's sometimes made with strawberry liqueur as a variation, which isn't quite as tasty. The wine of his district was made from Chardonnay grapes, which would make it an expensive tipple these days, but any dry white wine will do.

It's simple to make; simply pour five ounces of white wine, chilled, into a glass, add one ounce of cassis, and stir lightly. Cassis is rather sweet, so you may want to experiment with the proportion that's right for your taste.

A terrific variation of this is the Kir Royale, which uses Champagne and cassis in about the same proportions. The classic version of a cassis drink is the Vermouth Cassis, which is the same blend, using Dry Vermouth instead of white table wine.

SOL Y SOMBRE

In South America and Europe, they take
Vermouth seriously; in Argentina, what we call
the cocktail hour they call the Vermouth hour.

I learned about this drink from an Argen-
tinian who said it was very popular, but didn't
have a name; he called it "Sol y Sombre" —
sun and shade. Why not?

It is simply a mix of half Dry Vermouth
(sun) and half Sweet Vermouth (shade), with
a twist of lemon peel added. It's fine as is, but
many Americans seem to prefer it over a
couple of cubes of ice. Since Vermouths are
made with extensive blends of spices steeped
in the wine, it seems to me a shame to dilute
the delicate flavors; better to chill the bottles in
the refrigerator if you want to drink it cold.

GLOGG

There are probably as many mulled-wine
drinks as there are cold nights in Scandinavia.
Glogg is the best, but I wouldn't turn down
a cup of Gluwhein or a Bishop (red wine, Port
and spices) or any of the others.

   ¾ cup raisins
    1 tbsp. whole cardamon
    2 tsp. whole cloves
    1 stick cinnamon
 1½ cups water
    1 bottle (fifth) dry red wine
    ½ cup sugar
    ¼ cup blanched almonds

Rinse and drain the raisins, peel and crush the
cardamon. Combine the spices with half a cup
of raisins and water, and simmer half an hour.
Strain the liquid and add it to the wine. Stir
in the sugar and heat to just simmering for a
moment. Serve hot, with remaining raisins
and almonds in each cup.

MAY WINE BOWL

May wine is a delightful German idea — white wine flavored with woodruff, which has a spicy-sweet scent. They make up batches of it every spring, letting the herb steep in the wine till its spiciness pervades it.

Not much reaches our shores, and it doesn't seem to me quite as good as it used to be. Happily, it's easy to make your own, as a delightful Californian party punch. Use an inexpensive Riesling or even a fruity Chenin Blanc for the base wine. You can get woodruff in a gourmet shop or one that specializes in spices and teas.

½ package woodruff
6 bottles (fifths) white wine
1 bottle (fifth) Champagne
2 ounces brandy
¼ cup sugar
1 (10-oz.) bottle club soda

Soak woodruff overnight in one bottle of wine. Strain and mix with remaining wine, the Champagne and brandy. Dissolve sugar in club soda and add. Needless to say, all the ingredients except the club soda and sugar should have been well chilled in advance. If you like the taste of the woodruff, add the remainder of the package to the punch bowl. Serve with a fresh strawberry in each glass. Makes thirty servings.

BRIDE AND GROOM BOWL

    2 large limes
    4 oranges
    1 can (14 to 16 oz.) pitted dark sweet
      cherries
    1 bottle Chenin Blanc
    4 oz. brandy
    2 tbsp. superfine sugar
    1 bottle Champagne, chilled

Peel the oranges and limes in long spirals and
squeeze their juice into a two-quart pitcher.
Add the peels, cherries with their syrup,
Chenin Blanc and brandy. Cover and refrigerate. Before serving, add the sugar to the
mixture and stir till dissolved. Pour the punch
over ice in a punch bowl and add the
Champagne. Makes fifteen servings.

THE TOP 10 ───
WINE DISHES ───

People have been using wine in cookery since the time of the Egyptians, though it must be admitted that the early recipes were intended more as curatives or restoratives than *haute cuisine*. Its frequent use as a marinade probably dates back to the time when it was discovered that wine was an excellent preservative — and since the food always ends up tasting better, its popularity was assured.

Of course, there are few limitations on wine cookery, and you can easily invent dishes of your own. Just substitute wine for other liquid in any recipes you now use. Another neat trick is to pour an ounce or two of sherry into any soup as it's cooking (always add wine to a dish early in the game, so its flavor marries with the other ingredients as it cooks — if you add wine at the last minute, that's all you'll taste).

The alcohol (and therefore most of the calories) in wine vaporizes while the dish is cooking, so all you are left with is superb extra flavor. Wine is also an excellent tenderizer; marinate lean meat like flank steak in red wine for a few hours before cooking and you'll see the difference in texture as well as flavor.

All recipes listed here serve six.

POULET MARENGO

Napoleon was a notorious gourmand — he ate heavily, even on the battlefield, and he did so whenever he felt like it, which was often. (He also suffered from chronic indigestion, hardly surprising.) The story has it that the larder was bare after the Battle of Marengo, and that his chef scoured the countryside and came up with a chicken, some eggs, mushrooms, tomatoes and crayfish scooped up from a stream he waded, getting back to camp just in time to toss it all into a pot and create a dish Napoleon dubbed Poulet Marengo.

Our version is a little less frantically prepared, and that much the better for it. I'd serve it with a nice cold Chardonnay, or even a good Gamay Beaujolais.

3-lb. chicken, cut into serving pieces
1 onion, sliced
½ cup flour
1 tsp. salt
½ tsp. black pepper
½ tsp. tarragon
½ tsp. thyme
½ cup olive oil
1 cup white wine
½ cup chicken stock
2 cups quartered peeled tomatoes
2 cloves garlic, minced
8-10 mushrooms, sliced
1 cup pitted black olives
chopped parsley

Dredge chicken in flour mixed with salt, pepper, tarragon and thyme; save remaining flour. Saute onion in oil in a heavy skillet until transparent, then remove and set aside. Saute chicken in the oil until golden on all sides. Place chicken and onion in Dutch oven or other heavy pot.

Beat remaining flour mixture into the oil with a wire whisk, over low heat. Gradually add chicken stock, then wine, stirring constantly until smooth. Pour sauce over chicken and add mushrooms, tomatoes, olives and garlic. Cover and bake at 350 degrees for 45 minutes, or until chicken is tender. Garnish with chopped parsley and serve over brown rice. A nice touch would be to shell, devein and simmer a few shrimp and add them as an additional garnish.

CHOUCROUTE
A L'ALSACIENNE

As with many other classic dishes, Choucroute has many variations. All of them are good, I think. I prefer to wash the sauerkraut and drain it; you sacrifice some vitamin C that way, but you also get rid of some of the acidity, ending up with nicely balanced flavors. I also favor two kinds of meat, which makes it more interesting.

A fairly sturdy white wine is called for to go with it, and one of the best choices would be the spicy Gewurztraminer, which is what the Alsatians frequently choose.

    2 lbs. sauerkraut, canned or fresh
    ½-lb. bacon, cut in two-inch slices
    ½ cup chopped carrots
    1 onion, studded with cloves
    2 cloves minced garlic
    ¼ tsp. black pepper
    1 bay leaf
    white wine
    combination of meats

Drain sauerkraut and rinse with cold water in a colander for a few minutes. Toss well and let drain. Cook bacon about five minutes in Dutch oven or heavy pot, then add carrots and garlic. Saute for five minutes, then stir in sauerkraut. When well mixed, cover and let cook for five minutes over lowered heat.

Bury onion in sauerkraut, add pepper, bay leaf, and enough wine to cover. Simmer in the oven at 325 degrees about two hours, adding wine if necessary. Liquid should be absorbed before serving.

Meats: Polish or garlic sausages, knackwurst — one for each person. Cooked ham or roast pork — one slice each or two cups diced. Pork chops — one apiece. All should be added half an hour before the dish finishes cooking. Boiled, buttered potatoes are the perfect accompaniment.

FONDUE

Fondue is a friendly dish, a shared pleasure. Preceded by a tossed salad and accompanied by a bottle of dry white wine, it's also fit for kings. And queens. And friends.

An old Swiss custom has it that anyone who loses a piece of bread in the cheese has to kiss a member of the opposite sex at the table. This is one of the few Swiss customs that has persisted.

1 clove garlic
1 lb. gruyere cheese, coarsely grated
2 cups dry white wine
3 tbsp. kirsch liqueur
2 tsp. cornstarch
white pepper or nutmeg to taste

Rub a chafing dish with garlic. Add wine and heat until tiny bubbles form on the surface; do not boil. Add the cheese slowly, stirring constantly, until mixture just begins to thicken. Add the kirsch in which cornstarch has been dissolved and continue stirring until mixture bubbles. Season to taste with nutmeg or pepper.

Place chafing dish over low flame to serve; keep warm, but do not let the fondue simmer. Wine may be added if mixture becomes too thick. Serve with a basket of crusty French or Italian bread cut into one-inch squares.

BOEUF BOURGUIGNON

This dish really takes a whole day to come together, which makes it ideal for entertaining — simply refrigerate it overnight and reheat the next evening, and you can almost be a guest at your own dinner party.

Any red wine goes well with this, but it really deserves one of your best.

    2 lbs. lean beef, cubed
    2 cups dry red wine
    ½ lb. salt pork, sliced
    2 small onions, chopped
    2 shallots, chopped
    1 clove garlic, minced
    2 tbsp. oil
    1 cup carrots, diced
    ½ lb. mushrooms, chopped
    1½ tbsp. flour
    1 bay leaf
    ½ tsp. thyme
    ⅓ cup brandy
    salt and pepper to taste

Marinate beef overnight in wine to cover, refrigerated. When ready to cook, drain beef, reserving wine for later use in cooking. Saute salt pork, onions, shallots and garlic for about five minutes, then remove from pan. Saute beef in the fat until light brown. In the meantime, cover bottom of flameproof casserole with oil and carrots; transfer beef to casserole and add mushrooms. Sprinkle with flour, thyme, salt and pepper. Add bay leaf. Cover with salt pork, onions and shallots. Pour wine and brandy over all. Heat to boiling over a high flame. Immediately reduce heat and simmer, covered, for two to two-and-a-half hours. Serve over buttered egg noodles.

COQ AU VIN

Almost any wine will do for this simple dish, but red wine was the original choice, and still the best (I was once served chicken cooked in Lancer's Rosé, and it definitely left something to be desired).

For those who were brought up to think that only white wine goes with chicken, this dish might pose a problem; if they will view it as an opportunity to discover the versatility of wine, it will instead be a revelation. A light Zinfandel or Gamay Beaujolais, or even Pinot Noir would be a perfect choice in and with Coq au Vin.

> 4-5-lb. roasting chicken, cut into
>   serving pieces
> flour for dredging
> 3 tbsp. butter
> 2 tbsp. parsley, chopped
> 1 tbsp. marjoram
> 1 bay leaf
> ½ tsp. thyme
> ¼-lb. salt pork, chopped
> 10 pearl onions, peeled
> 1 carrot, chopped
> 3 shallots, chopped
> 1 clove garlic, minced
> ½-lb. mushrooms, sliced
> 1½ cups dry red wine
>   salt and pepper to taste

Lightly dredge chicken in flour. Saute salt pork, onions, carrot, shallots and garlic in butter for a few minutes. Remove and saute chicken until a golden brown. Place chicken and vegetables in a heavy casserole. Add parsley, marjoram, bay leaf, salt and pepper. Add wine. Cover and bake at 300 degrees for two hours. Add mushrooms for the last ten minutes of cooking. Serve chicken with vegetables and sauce poured over it.

BEEF STROGANOFF

This is one of the lovely reminders that there is (or was, anyway) such a thing as Russian cuisine, though it's one of the few Russian dishes I know of made with wine.

It is so rich that it calls for an equally rich red wine to accompany it, such as a Cabernet Sauvignon, or a big Zinfandel or Petite Sirah.

1½ lbs. beef fillet
3 tbsp. butter
flour for dredging
1 tbsp. grated onion
8 mushrooms, sliced
1 tsp. prepared mustard
½ tsp. basil
¼ cup white wine
1 cup sour cream
salt and pepper to taste

Remove sour cream from refrigeator; it is important that it be close to room temperature. Slice beef ½-inch thick and pound slices out. Cut into strips. Dredge beef strips in flour seasoned with salt and pepper. Saute onion in one tablespoon of butter for two minutes, then add beef and saute another five minutes. Remove beef and onions to a hot plate. Saute mushrooms in remaining two tablespoons of butter. Return beef and onions to skillet and add mustard, basil and wine. Stir thoroughly for a few minutes then, off the heat, stir in sour cream. Let heat up but do not boil, as sauce will separate. Serve over buttered egg noodles.

VITELLO TONNATO

If you just read the ingredients for this recipe, you might just think it was the darndest thing you'd ever heard of and promptly forget about it. But you'd be missing something quite terrific.

A Zinfandel or Barbera is the perfect accompaniment.

Veal:
2½-3-lb. boneless rolled leg of veal
2 carrots
3 sprigs parsley
2 bay leaves
1 large onion
2 celery stalks
¼ tsp. thyme
pepper to taste
Sauce:

1 cup mayonnaise	3 tbsp. capers
1 seven-oz. can tuna	salt to taste
1 two-oz. can anchovy fillets	
1 cup olive oil	
½ cup dry white wine	
3 tbsp. lemon juice	

Veal: Add all ingredients but veal to enough water to cover the veal in a heavy kettle or Dutch oven. Bring to a boil and add the veal. When the water comes to the second boil, cover tightly and reduce heat. Simmer gently for two hours. Allow meat to cool in its own broth, then chill.

Sauce: Mix tuna, anchovies, olive oil, wine and capers. Puree in a food processor or blender until creamy. Fold mixture into the mayonnaise. Salt, if necessary, to taste.

Slice chilled veal thinly and arrange alternating layers of sauce and meat on a platter.

Refrigerate, covered loosely by foil, for at least twenty-four hours. Garnish platter with olives, capers and sprigs of parsley.

COQUILLES ST. JACQUES

This classic shellfish dish is one that everyone knows but few prepare. Served gratineed in individual scallop shells, it is an impressive dinner-party dish, especially when served with a chilled Chardonnay, which complements it exactly.

1½ lbs. scallops	4 tbsp. butter
10 mushrooms, sliced	¼ cup flour
6 shallots, chopped	¾ cup milk
bouquet garni	3 egg yolks
1½ cups dry white wine	1 cup whipping cream
6 tbsp. butter	½ cup grated
½ tsp. salt	Parmesan cheese
pinch of pepper	½ cup bread crumbs
juice of 1 lemon	

Simmer wine, shallots, bouquet garni, salt and pepper for five minutes. Wash scallops well; if they are large sea scallops, cut in half. Add scallops, mushrooms and 2 tablespoons of butter, and simmer slowly for four minutes; you may need to add some wine to insure that the scallops are covered. Remove scallops and mushrooms from broth and set aside; reserve liquid. Discard bouquet garni. When scallops are cool, cut into small pieces. Reserve the broth.

Make a roux with three tablespoons of butter and a scant quarter-cup of flour. Add the broth used to simmer the scallops slowly, then the milk, beating with a wire whisk. Add scallops and mushrooms and heat in sauce, but do not let boil. Combine egg yolks and cream and blend into mixture. Stir over low heat till well thickened. Spoon into buttered scallop shells or individual casseroles. Sprinkle with bread crumbs and cheese and dot with butter. Arrange on a broiling pan and run under a broiler for a few minutes, until top is brown.

SOLE FLORENTINE

Fish and wine go together like ham and
eggs, Laurel and Hardy — you name it.
Marinating fish in wine for an hour before
cooking gives it an extra-special flavor, too.
Here's one of hundreds of variations on fish
and wine, which would go quite well with
Sauvignon Blanc or Chardonnay.

    2 lbs. spinach
    salt and pepper to taste
    ½ tsp. mace
    6 sole fillets
    6 tbsp. parsley, chopped
    ½ cup grated Swiss cheese
    Sauce:
    3 tbsp. butter
    6 tbsp. flour
    ⅔ cup milk
    ¼ cup white wine

Wash spinach well and remove stems; drain
and chop finely. Add salt and pepper to taste,
and mace. Spoon into buttered baking dish.
Sprinkle fillets with salt and parsley and roll
them up. Arrange the rolls on top of spinach.
Make a roux with butter and flour, add milk
and stir as it thickens; add wine and let it
simmer till smooth. Pour the sauce over the
fish, sprinkle with the cheese and bake in a
350-degree oven for about twenty-five minutes.

CHAMPAGNE AND STRAWBERRIES

After making a full meal, it is probably best for the hostess as well as the guests to have a light and simple dessert. This is my favorite, no less elegant for being easy.

1 pound strawberries
1 bottle Brut Champagne
6 tbsp. superfine sugar

Wash and de-stem strawberries, place several in the bottom of oversize wine glasses (at least fourteen ounces). Sprinkle one tablespoon sugar into each glass. Add Champagne and serve with long spoons; guests eat the strawberries and then drink the Champagne.

If strawberries are out of season, many other fruits will do as well, especially peaches. If fresh fruits are unavailable, frozen or canned will do, but skip the sugar and only include half of any syrup.

THE TOP 10
CHEESE & WINE MATCH-UPS

There is not just an affinity with wine and cheese — it's a marriage. Perhaps it's because both depend on yeast for their fermentations, perhaps because the best cheeses have the same sort of flavor complexities as the best wines. At any rate, they say in the wine trade, "Buy on bread, sell on cheese," as cheese improves the flavor of any wine.

It is a sad fact that in America, with all our bounty, we don't have or get the best cheeses in the world. Our domestic cheeses, in too many cases, are compromised by a need to reach a mass market, so the flavors are toned town. And many foreign cheeses are heavily salted to increase their shelf life; additionally, the Food and Drug Administration has some peculiar notions about its duty to protect us, so some natural flavorings are not allowed in cheese meant for export to the U.S.

Of course, there are a lot of cheeses available (when Churchill was told France made over 350 types of cheese, he declared that such a place had to be ungovernable). These ten are among the world's best, and not found in bulk, so you may need to search them out at a specialty shop. I promise you it is worth the trouble; imitation prevails in the cheese business, but it is rarely sincere and never flattering.

BRIE. Easily one of the best cheeses in the world, but many Americans are put off by it because they think of it as too strong — probably they have had it too many times past its prime. Brie should be plump and slightly yielding to the touch, with the pale yellow color of fresh sweet butter inside; once cut, a wheel of Brie will not continue to ripen well or uniformly, so it is best saved for company, when a wheel or wedge can be eaten at once. Canned versions are usually awful; domestic versions tend to be somewhat oversalted. The best of the American versions is by a California company called Rouge et Noir. Companion: Cabernet Sauvignon.

CAMEMBERT. Supposedly, the first time Napoleon was served this cheese, he kissed the waitress who brought it. It was the least he could do, I think; he also named it. A cousin of Brie, a little more common but no less good. In France, it is made with unpasteurized milk, and superb; the export version is simply very, very good. Like Brie, it should be plump and slightly yielding, and the edible rind should be white or slightly off-white; spots of tan on the rind, sagging in the middle and a wisp of ammonia will tell you it's over the hill. With both these cheeses, it's best to buy them slightly underripe a few days (very few) before you plan to serve them. Remove from refrigerator half an hour before serving to allow them to come to cool room temperature. As with Brie, there are dreadful canned versions around; domestically, Rouge et Noir also makes a decent version of Camembert. Pair it with Cabernet or a good Pinot Noir.

STILTON. Of all the blue cheeses, Stilton may be the greatest; it is certainly the best we can get in America, as many Roqueforts are terribly uneven in quality due to oversalting. Not only is it made from rich milk, but cream is added in the early stage, giving the ripened cheese a mellow and rich undertone without the pungency of other blues. Port and Stilton is the most famous combination, but any big and robust red goes well with it, especially some of the newer big and fruity Petite Sirahs and Zinfandels.

CHEDDAR. It may come as a surprise to you, but Cheddar cheese is also a victim of politics; the English are not allowed to export it to America. The name has become meaningless over the years, however, so the only thing left is to sort among what we do have available. Vermont cheddar is white, sharp and utterly delicious, probably the best domestic we have. Canadian cheddar, distinguished by a black wax coat, is dark yellow, crumbly and sinfully rich; not the small bars some supermarkets sell, but the wheels you find in shops. Most other cheddars are made with pasteurized milk and end up either too bland or bitter. Any reasonably sturdy red wine goes well with Vermont or Canadian.

EMMENTHAL. This is Swiss cheese, imitated around the world and still unequalled. Beware of stores that advertise or otherwise push "imported Swiss;" there are thoroughly lousy versions from many countries sold in the U.S. Don't buy a hunk without asking to see the wheel it was cut from, for the distinct flavor of Emmenthal, slightly sweet with an under-tone of walnuts, is incomparable. Some Gruyeres are in the same sort of flavor zone, but not the prepackaged ones in supermarkets. Another beauty is Appenzel, cured with cider or white wine in its early stages, and very piquant. Any red will do with them, but a nice flavor combination can be made with a dry white, either a Fumé Blanc or Chardonnay.

MONTEREY JACK. Connoisseurs sometimes dismiss this cheese as an American Meunster, semisoft and bland, but they probably haven't had some of the fine-tuned versions being made by conscientious dairies here. Supermarket versions are sprouting all over the place, and they are indeed dull and bland; but if you get to know your friendly cheese-seller, he might get you some of the good and buttery Montereys that come out between Fall and Spring when cows fatten on fresh grass — the sweetness is hinted at in the cheese. Good with French bread, Chenin Blanc and even Rosé.

GOURMANDISE. This white and creamy cheese is distinguished by pictures of cherries, and lately other fruits, on its wrapping, and by its creaminess and sweetness. Authentic gourmandise is flavored with kirsch (it's frequently called "kirsch cheese"), but the version we get here (thanks, FDA) is flavored with cherry extract. Other flavors have lately been introduced, and the best that can be said about them is that they're not bad. A good dessert cheese, goes nicely with a cool and crisp Johannisberg Riesling and Anjou pears.

EDAM and GOUDA. Like too many other cheeses, these have been given a bad name by all the imitations that flood the supermarket cases. The real thing, from Holland, proves to be something else, somewhat bland but wholesome and a good combiner with other foods (the Dutch like them with paper-thin slices of ham and buttered pumpernickel bread). Edam has the bright red rind and is made from partly skim milk; Gouda has a yellow rind and is made from whole milk. They also make agreeable companions to any wines.

BEL PAESE. Buttery and delicately flavored, this Italian cheese is one of the most dependable. Its package, with the map of Italy and portrait of Antonio Stoppani (who was an author, priest, and friend of the original cheesemaker), is seen everywhere now, and has spawned a slightly inferior domestic version — the map is of America, not Italy. It is delightfully creamy and agreeably tart in the aftertaste, and a good match for any dry wine.

HAVARTI. There is Havarti and Havarti. The best ones are the double-cream versions found in specialty shops, from Denmark; they are like fresh sweet butter, melting in your mouth, and sinfully rich, though delicately flavored. The ordinary version is, well, ordinary. Good with Zinfandel and other lighter red wines.

THE TOP 10
WINE QUOTES

There is something about wine that brings out the poet in people; maybe it's just because it is as delightful as it is undefinable. About half of what has been written about wine is either silly, pompous or both. Hilaire Belloc, for example, once wrote a "heroic poem" on the subject, and I don't know anybody who ever finished reading the thing.

Other people had more luck expressing themselves. Here are ten of them.

"Drink wine and you will sleep well. Sleep well and you will not sin. Avoid sin, and you will be saved. Ergo, drink wine and be saved."

> —Usually attributed to Martin Luther, but more likely the work of a scurrilous satirist

"Drink a glass of wine after your soup, and you steal a ruble from the doctor."

> —Old Russian proverb

"Wine is constant proof that God loves us and loves to see us happy."

> —Benjamin Franklin

"Three are the things I shall never attain — Envy, content, and sufficient Champagne."

> —Dorothy Parker

"There are two reasons for drinking wine: one is, when you are thirsty, to cure it; the other, when you are not thirsty, to prevent it. Prevention is always better than cure."

> —Thomas Love Peacock

". . . and the wine is bottled poetry."

—Robert Louis Stevenson

"You Americans have the loveliest wines in the world, you know, but you don't realize it. You call them 'domestic,' and that's enough to start trouble anywhere."

—H.G. Wells

"God in his goodness sent the grapes,
To cheer both great and small.
Little fools will drink too much,
And great fools none at all."

—Anonymous

"There are more old wine drinkers than old doctors."

—German proverb

"Fish without wine is like an egg without salt."

—Auguste Escoffier

TOASTS FOR MOST OCCASIONS

The term "toast" is said to come from the ancient custom of putting a piece of toast in each wine glass for the first round. Possibly it was a form of secular communion.

At the same time, in those rough-and-ready medieval days, the host was expected to rise and say something, if not eloquent, then at least friendly. Thus "a toast" was born. I think all of us who aren't great ad-libbers have to admire the first fellow who thought of "Here's to you!" to get through it quickly.

"May the hinges of friendship never rust, or the wings of love never lose a feather."

—Old Scottish toast

"Here's to health, money and love — and the time to enjoy them."

—from the Spanish

"With wine and hope, anything is possible."

—old Spanish toast

"Let us have wine and women, mirth and laughter,
    Sermons and soda-water the day after."

—Lord Byron

"Fan the flame of hilarity with the wing of friendship, and pass the rosy wine."

—Charles Dickens

"Though youth gave love and roses,
    Age still leaves us friends and wine."

—Thomas Moore

"He who clinks his cup with mine,
    Adds a glory to the wine."

—George Sterling